INTERNATIONAL PUBLIC SECTOR ACCOUNTING STANDARDS IMPLEMENTATION ROAD MAP FOR UZBEKISTAN

NOVEMBER 2023

ASIAN DEVELOPMENT BANK

ADB

6 ADB Avenue, Mandaluyong City, 1550 Metro Manila, Philippines
Tel +63 2 8632 4444; Fax +63 2 8636 2444
www.adb.org

ISBN 978-92-9270-286-1 (print); 978-92-9270-287-8 (electronic); 978-92-9270-288-5 (ebook)
Publication Stock No. TCS230470
DOI: http://dx.doi.org/10.22617/TCS230470

Note:
In this publication, "$" refers to United States dollars.

Cover design by Claudette Rodrigo.

This report was prepared by AARC Ltd (Consultant) under the ADB technical assistance project: Strengthening Financial Management in Asia and the Pacific, Phase 2. This report is published by ADB under the technical assistance project Public Sector Accounting Standards (Eighth Phase).

CONTENTS

TABLES, FIGURES, AND BOX

Tables

Figures

Box

ABBREVIATIONS

ADB	–	Asian Development Bank
COA	–	chart of accounts
CRU	–	Control and Revision Unit (Financial Inspection Service of the Ministry of Finance)
FTE	–	full-time equivalent
GFS	–	government financial statistics
GGS	–	general government sector
IFMIS	–	integrated financial management information system
IFRS	–	international financial reporting standards
IMF	–	International Monetary Fund
IPSAS	–	International Public Sector Accounting Standards
IPSASB	–	International Public Sector Accounting Standards Board
ISPFM	–	information system for public financial management
IT	–	information technology
M&E	–	monitoring and evaluation
MOF	–	Ministry of Finance
NAS	–	national accounting standards
NPSAS	–	National Public Sector Accounting Standards
PEFA	–	public expenditure and financial accountability
PFM	–	public financial management
PMU	–	Project Management Unit
SOE	–	state-owned enterprise
STF	–	state targets fund
UCOA	–	unified chart of accounts
UZASBO	–	Uzbekistan Automated System for Budget Organizations

INTRODUCTION AND OVERVIEW OF THE REPORT

1

1.1 Introduction

Uzbekistan's Ministry of Finance (MOF) has accepted this road map as a guide to implementing International Public Sector Accounting Standards (IPSAS), under its Economic Management Improvement Program, effective since December 2019.

The Asian Development Bank (ADB) financed a technical assistance project to develop this road map and advise until its finalization. Aiming to advance the MOF's progress already made in this direction, the project began when 12 national accounting standards (NAS), based on accrual IPSAS, were scheduled to be implemented. The MOF planned to disseminate these new standards to accountants, and make any necessary revisions to enabling legislative instruments.[1]

1.2 Document Structure

This report contains the following sections:

Section 1: **Introduction and Overview of the Report.** Provides an overview of the road map.

Section 2: **Detailed Phases of the Road Map.** Highlights all the necessary details of the suggested work content and timing of the four phases of the road map.

Section 3: **Objectives and Status of the Project.** Important background information to the road map, including the status of recent public financial management (PFM) reform initiatives.

Section 4: **Implementation Phasing and Development of the Chart of Accounts.** Presents a suggested phasing for implementing new accounting standards and considers the development of the chart of accounts (COA).

Section 5: **Consolidated Financial Reporting for the Public Sector.** Shows why it is necessary to consider consolidating different sources of financial reporting to arrive at a general government- or public sector-wide view of financial performance and position.

Section 6: **Project Management and Risks.** Outlines the project management structures and processes, the role of audit, and the project's key risks.

---

1 MOF. *Action Plan for the Harmonization of Accounting with International Public Sector Accounting Standards (IPSAS) 2018–2020.* Tashkent [*План мероприятий по гармонизации порядка бюджетного учета с Международными стандартами финансовой отчетности в государственном секторе* (IPSAS) *на 2018–2020 годы*].

1.3 Key Aspects of International Public Sector Accounting Standards Implementation in Uzbekistan

1.3.1 The Long Road to Accounting Reform

Adopting a new public sector accounting regime is never easy: unified public financial reporting on a national scale is inevitably a reform that unfolds, at best over the medium term, but usually over the long term. And so it is expected that despite the considerable attempts already made by the Government of Uzbekistan to develop the foundations for a more robust PFM environment, introducing a full IPSAS financial reporting framework will probably take at least a decade, even with the political will of the government behind it.

However, key milestones may be set along the road to this seemingly distant destination. Some countries, for example, adopt cash-basis IPSAS as an expedient measure on the journey to full accrual IPSAS.. In the case of Uzbekistan, the country's long-term PFM policy states that interim progress will be signposted by the phased introduction of NAS based on accrual IPSAS. This road map refers to these standards as National Public Sector Accounting Standards (NPSAS).[2] The key steps in the IPSAS Implementation Road Map proposed in this report are summarized in the following subsections.

1.3.2 The Need to Consolidate Public Sector Financial Reporting

The government's existing accounting reform plan prescribes that financial reporting under NPSAS should coincide with the consolidated budget. However, the actual scope of IPSAS financial reporting is determined by whether the government controls public sector entities directly or indirectly. To achieve whole-of-public sector accounting, government sector entities often must be consolidated with public corporations reporting under International Financial Reporting Standards (IFRS).[3] Thus, consolidation of the financial results prepared under compatible but different frameworks is a long-term, if not necessarily permanent, feature of the public sector financial reporting landscape.

With the state-owned enterprises (SOEs) already applying NAS (based on IFRS), it may be difficult in the short or medium term to require a relatively large number of SOEs to adopt an IPSAS-based framework in the early stages of its development. It should be recognized, too, that the formats of the SOEs' existing financial statements are different in several key respects from those proposed for NPSAS financial reporting and even from IPSAS reports. Nevertheless, a method will have to be found to map all public sector entities' financial results and positions within the scope of IPSAS to a set of consolidated reports.

---

[2] The MOF mostly refers to these standards as budgeting accounting standards (*СБУ – Стандарты бюджетного учета*) but also, on occasions, to standards of accounting (*Стандарты бухгалтерского учета*). This confusion stems from a lack of embedded understanding of the role IPSAS plays in defining best practice in financial reporting as opposed to the established norms of budget accounting.

[3] IFRS are primarily developed for use by private sector entities but are also widely used internationally as the accounting framework for public corporations with a profit motive. Recent guidance from the International Public Sector Accounting Standards Board (IPSASB) makes clear, however, that IPSAS should be used for not-for-profit SOEs; see IPSASB. 2016. *The Applicability of IPSASs.*

1.4 The Road Map

The IPSAS Implementation Road Map for Uzbekistan is divided into four phases. Public sector entities in the country will have developed the ability to prepare financial statements in compliance with accruals IPSAS. The first three phases use adapted national standards based on IPSAS to progressively build the financial reporting capacity of the reporting entities until, in phase 4, Uzbekistan leaves behind the NPSAS framework developed during the first 6 years of the road map schedule and, over the following 5 years, proceeds to the implementation of IPSAS (Figure 1). The NPSAS would be retired, and the full IPSAS framework would be adopted in its place.

Figure 1: The Transition to International Public Sector Accounting Standards via National Public Sector Accounting Standards

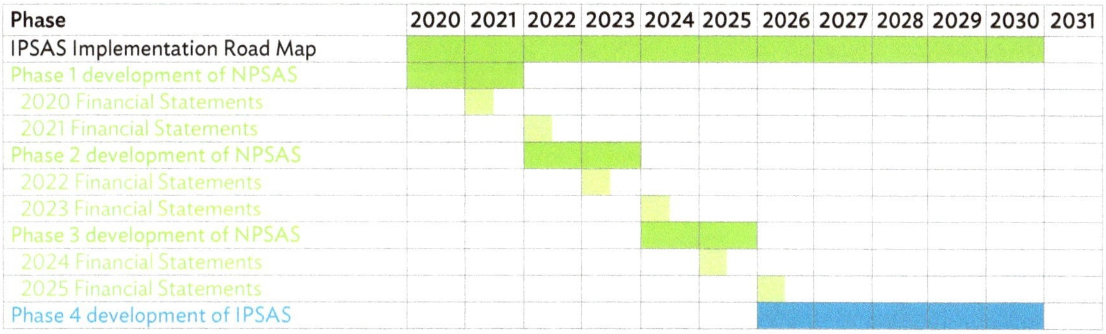

IPSAS = International Public Sector Accounting Standards, NPSAS = National Public Sector Accounting Standards.
Source: Consultant's analysis.

As the IPSAS framework requires an "all or nothing" implementation, the transition to phase 4 will only be contemplated when it is deemed that public sector financial reporting in Uzbekistan is sufficiently mature to cope with the demands of full IPSAS.

1.4.1 Phases of International Public Sector Accounting Standards Implementation

The road map recommends phased measures over at least a decade:

- **Phase 1 (2020)** will be based on the existing 12 NPSAS with some proposed changes, as discussed in section 4. Necessary refinements of the COA and information technology (IT) systems will be made in support of these new NPSAS. The intended scope of the implementation by the end of this phase is the consolidated budget that encompasses all budget organizations plus state targets funds (STFs) and subnational government entities.
- **Phase 2 (2021–2022)** would encourage the application of IPSAS-based financial reporting by as many entities as possible within the general government sector (complying with the government financial statistics [GFS] requirements of the International Monetary Fund [IMF] and leading toward implementation of IPSAS 22), primarily noncommercial SOEs. Further NPSASs will be developed and introduced in this period.

Regardless of the final decision about coverage, for all entities in the scope of NPSAS, the concept of fair value is to be embedded in revised and newly adapted standards and relevant accounting and reporting methodologies.

- **Phase 3 (2023–2024)** will seek to adapt further IPSAS for use in Uzbekistan.

  Expanding the coverage of NPSAS toward the full scope of IPSAS may continue the transitional arrangements under phase 2, depending on political support for this idea.

- **Phase 4 (2025–2030)** is when the relevant authorities in Uzbekistan may consider disseminating a new medium-term transition plan and relevant enabling legislation for the adoption of IPSAS as the only financial reporting framework in use for public sector entities other than those "commercial SOEs" that seek a profit. At this point, IPSAS 33 (first-time adoption) is used, although it should be referred to as guidance on phasing implementation early in the process.

  The point of transition to full IPSAS from the beginning of phase 4 of the road map may only be achievable once the necessary know-how from consolidating accrual financial reporting under NPSAS over the previous three phases and changes to the coverage of NPSAS financial reporting (embracing noncommercial SOEs and, if possible and appropriate, transferring noncommercial SOEs to NPSAS from the current NAS compliant with IFRS) has been firmly established.

  Public interest entities and other commercial state-owned corporations would continue to report under NAS or IFRS. They include whole-of-public sector reporting via a consolidation process facilitated by aligning accounting policies between IPSAS- and IFRS-adopting reporting entities.

1.4.2 *Information Technology and Chart of Accounts Interventions*

The road map also contains actions to provide new IT system functionalities and changes to the unified chart of accounts (UCOA) to enable the implementation of the NPSAS and IPSAS financial reporting frameworks (Figure 2). Further details are included in sections 2 and 3.

The overall timeline and content of the IPSAS Implementation Road Map is given in Table 1.

Figure 2: Information Technology System and Chart of Accounts Amendment Milestones

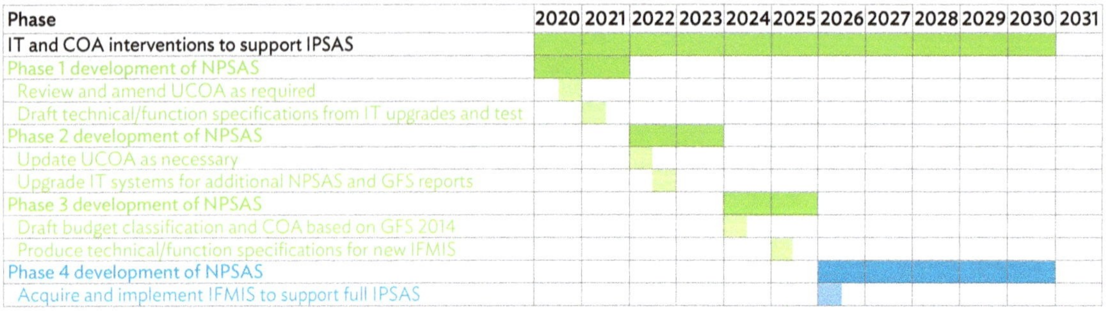

COA = chart of accounts, GFS = government financial statistics, IFMIS = integrated financial management information system, IPSAS = International Public Sector Accounting Standards, IT = information technology, NPSAS = National Public Sector Accounting Standards, UCOA = unified chart of accounts.

Source: Consultant's analysis.

Table 1: The Transition to International Public Sector Accounting Standards via National Public Sector Accounting Standards—Road Map for International Public Sector Accounting Standards Implementation

	NPSAS and Regulations	Accounting, COA and IT	Training and Communication	Financial Reports	Risk and Mitigation
Phase 1 2020–2021	• Set up PMU and Steering Committee • Initial batch of NPSAS put in place • Draft consolidation rules based on IPSAS 35 and NPSAS equivalent • Update implementation guidance • Change regulations to implement new accounting and reporting	• Review and amend UCOA as required • Draft detailed consolidation rules • More of government debt recognized and measured than hitherto • Draft functional specification for IT upgrades and system volume test	• Run awareness program for all stakeholders including politicians • Train staff of MOF, budget organizations, SAI in NPSAS • Set up user help desk • Form M&E unit at MOF • Put e-learning materials online	• Develop in NPSAS 3 new financial report formats in line with IPSAS 1, 2 and 24, suitable for publication • More debt accrued on balance sheets of the entities in scope • Verify reports properly generated from UCOA and IT systems	• *Risk 1:* Changes to the Road Map schedule or scope *Mitigation:* Strong project management and political support • *Risk 2:* Resistance to change from politicians and officials *Mitigation:* High-level political support, consultation, and communication • *Risk 3:* Staff unable to perform new tasks *Mitigation:* Testing systems and training, help desk • *Risk 4:* Procedures, UCOA and/or IT systems unable to provide required reports *Mitigation:* Comprehensive testing and revising as required • *Risk 5:* Inadequate management of change and new procedures *Mitigation:* Establishment of dedicated PMU with sufficient authority to manage reforms across government • *Risk 6:* IPSAS coverage is limited to the consolidated budget due to government policy for PFM *Mitigation:* Ensure that financial reports for the whole of the public sector are consolidated • *Risk 7:* Decision-makers use the improved information ineffectively *Mitigation:* Awareness-building sessions and guidance for users
Phase 2 2022–2023	• Adapt additional NPSAS, consider relevant NAS accounting policies • Review existing NPSAS to ensure continuing IPSAS convergence • Extend implementation guidance to cover additional NPSAS • SOES to be classified as part of GGS or public corporations	• Extend scope of consolidation to whole of general government sector • Test understanding of consolidations • Update UCOA as necessary • Upgrade IT systems for additional or revised NPSAS and GFS	• Train staff at SOEs required to implement new UCOA, IT systems, and consolidation • Train practitioner, MOF, and audit staff in new NPSAS and implementation guidance • Update e-learning materials	• Financial reports of NPSAS entities for 2021 and 2022 are in line with IPSAS, including debt accruals • Comparative figures incorporated in financial reports • Consolidation rules are applied • Develop GFS reports	
Phase 3 2024–2025	• Adapt all remaining key IPSAS into NPSAS with new implementation guidance, considering relevant accounting policies in NAS • Update existing NPSAS to converge with remaining corresponding IPSAS	• Extend the scope of NPSAS further • Prepare a register of all fiscal risks • Implement procedures for new and amended NPSAS • Test success of consolidation process • Change regulations to implement	• Extend the scope of NPSAS further • Prepare a register of all fiscal risks • Implement procedures for new and amended NPSAS • Test success of consolidation process • Change regulations to implement	• All debt assets, liabilities, and guarantees reflected in the balance sheets of government entities • Incorporate contingent liabilities and third-party payments into financial reports • Continue comparative analysis	
Phase 4 2026–2030	• Adopt IPSAS for the public sector except for entities applying IFRS • Implement regulations requiring public corporations to adopt IFRS but provide information for consolidation	• Implement upgraded or new IT systems to handle all IPSAS and GFS reporting requirements • Revise accounting procedures for new requirements • Implement new IFMIS	• Run comprehensive IPSAS training programs for key staff • Consolidate all previous learning • Verify the status of user knowledge • Update e-learning materials	• Prepare financial statements including disclosures that are fully compliant with IPSAS • Enable GFS reporting in accordance with IMF requirements • Whole of public sector financial reporting is finally made possible	

COA = chart of accounts, GFS = government financial statistics, GGS = general government sector, IFMIS = integrated financial management information system, IFRS = international financial reporting standards, IPSAS = International Public Sector Accounting Standards, IT = information technology, M&E = monitoring and evaluation, MOF = Ministry of Finance, NAS = national accounting standards, NPSAS = National Public Sector Accounting Standards, PMU = Project Management Unit, SAI = Supreme Audit Institution, SOE = state-owned enterprise, UCOA = unified chart of accounts.

Source: Consultant's analysis.

2 DETAILED PHASES OF THE ROAD MAP

2.1 Phase 1 Actions

Table 2: Phase 1 Actions

Start Point of the Phase	Standards and Regulatory Framework Actions	Reporting, Accounting, COA, and IT Actions	Training and Other Actions	End Point of the Phase
Beginning of 2020	2020–2021			End of 2021
• Initial batch of NPSAS is ready for adoption • PMU is set up • M&E / help-desk capability is identified	• NPSAS 3 is updated with new reporting formats • Two NPSAS are deferred, one may be withdrawn, three new NPSAS are developed per the road map schedule (NAS accounting policies should be considered) • The IPSAS conceptual framework is adopted as a regulating document • Consolidation rules based on IPSAS 35 are developed, and the drafting of a new NPSAS begins accordingly • Regulatory changes to enable new accounting and reporting requirements are made	• NPSAS 3 financial reports published in 2020 for 2019 • Further Standards concerning reporting (IPSASs 2 and 24) will be added • New IPSAS-style reporting formats are developed for the financial results and position of the 2020 financial year and onward • Recognition and measurement of debt assets and liabilities are prioritized • Necessary changes to IT systems and COA are specified and coded to enable amended accounting and reporting requirements	• NPSAS awareness-raising events are held • NPSAS training plan and materials for MOF officials, auditors, and senior accountants in the reporting entities are developed and disseminated • PMU and M&E resources begin to function. Help-desk phoneline in place • E-learning training materials made available to practitioners and auditors • Carry out tactical recruitment of new accounting graduates	• A total of 15 NPSAS (the 12 already drafted plus three NPSAS based on IPSAS 2, 24, and 35) are developed and primarily, if not entirely, implemented • Interested parties have a more developed awareness of consolidation rules • Inventory of SOEs (not managed by the project) has concluded that market/nonmarket SOEs which should therefore use NAS/NPSAS, respectively

COA = chart of accounts, IPSAS = International Public Sector Accounting Standards, IT = information technology, M&E = monitoring and evaluation, MOF = Ministry of Finance, NAS = national accounting standards, NPSAS = National Public Sector Accounting Standards, PMU = Project Management Unit, SOE = state-owned enterprise.

Source: Consultant's analysis.

2.1.1 Starting Point of Phase 1

Before the start of the phase in January 2020, a Project Management Unit (PMU) should be set up and work alongside the Department for Methodology and Introduction of Treasury Execution for the State Budget (Budget Organizations' Methodology Department). Initially, this may consist of at least one full-time equivalent (FTE) who is suitably experienced and knowledgeable about the scope and direction of accounting reform and with sufficient proven knowledge of accounting and financial reporting, preferably backed by professional qualifications or experience, to be able to take the technical lead from the MOF's side on matters relating to the amendment or drafting of NPSAS. More human and financial resources could be added to the PMU as the volume and complexity of the workload increased during the implementation.

The MOF should also create and fund a help-desk telephone or online support function. This new function may physically be part of the existing IT support infrastructure within the MOF but has the necessary accounting knowledge to answer questions appropriately.

The centralized help-desk function should be seen as a permanent unit within the MOF charged with providing accountants at the budget organizations and STFs (initially) with timely, competent advisory support on the correct application of NPSAS throughout the IPSAS implementation period. The details of how this relatively small help function can be set up and how it will work with the various levels of government to help implement NPSAS will be worked out in the first half of phase 1.

2.1.2 Standards and Regulatory Framework

During this phase, the PMU (on behalf of the MOF) and the international and national consultants required to assist the MOF will confirm which additional standards (see section 4) should be added to the framework so that the new standards can regulate budget organizations' financial reporting from 2020 onward. The IPSAS conceptual framework should be translated into Uzbek and spread via a ministerial order as an official document regulating financial reporting under NPSAS, as it will give important guidance as to the fundamental principles to be applied.

In developing all new NPSAS standards, the MOF should consider the accounting policies in NAS in each relevant area so that the policies under NPSAS are as consistent with NAS as possible. This will minimize avoidable differences between the financial reports of SOEs and the budget sector and facilitate consolidation in the future.

For each new standard developed, relevant and appropriately detailed implementation guidance should be drawn up by the PMU and expert consultants partially within the standards and in the form of separate, more detailed explanatory material. Moreover, the MOF is currently in the process of revising the relevant instruction regulating financial reporting by budget entities, and it is anticipated that the project will help to supervise the delivery of these revisions so that they are fully aligned with the financial reporting requirements under NPSAS.[4]

[4] MOF Order #2169—on the Approval of Accounting Instructions for Budget Organizations (*Об утверждении инструкции по бухгалтерскому учету в бюджетных организациях*).

The principles of the consolidation scope and eliminating inter-entity flows should form the basis of detailed procedural instructions on consolidation based on IPSAS 35, which in turn should be used to specify the required IT system upgrades and define the training programs. Any changes arising during the phase to the formats of financial reports or disclosures for the organizations within the scope of NPSAS will need to be introduced in a revised version of NPSAS 3.

The new NPSAS also needs to be enabled and supported by government regulations. Other regulation changes may be required to implement the new reporting formats and clarify the respective financial reporting obligations of budget organizations, STFs, and SOEs.

2.1.3 Reporting and Accounting Actions

The financial reports to be used for 2019 will be those stated in the existing version of NPSAS 3, but during 2020, proposals for changes to the formats of NPSAS reports for financial years 2020 and beyond will be made. The content and format of future financial reports, including the type of disclosures normally expected under IPSAS, will need to be further developed to be as feasible to the financial statements listed in IPSAS 1.

For example, cash flow (based on IPSAS 2) and comparison of actuals with budget statements (based on IPSAS 24) will need to be added to the current list of prescribed reports. Consideration should also be given to using the financial information in the IT systems to generate GFS reports directly.

2.1.4 Chart of Accounts and Information Technology Systems Actions

The UCOA used to combine budget and financial reporting should also be subject to a detailed review by the implementation team during phase 1 to ensure that it meets the reporting requirements of the NPSAS and GFS and can be implemented through the IT systems.

The detailed procedural instructions for consolidation of the budget entities' financial reports based on IPSAS 35 should be used to specify the IT system upgrades required to deliver the prescribed results. This includes developing the capability to automatically identify and eliminate flows and balances between entities within the consolidation.

2.1.5 Training and Other Actions

An essential requirement is to make stakeholders across government, including politicians, aware of the ongoing changes and how the improved transparency will impact their roles and functions. This may be achieved through a dedicated website, printed newsletters, seminars, and ensuring appropriate media coverage. Civil society groups should also be involved in the awareness training.

A comprehensive training and recruitment plan should be implemented based on a full training needs analysis. It should set out the plan for appropriate training for different groups with different roles, for example, MOF accounting and methodological guidance staff, accounting staff in budget organizations, internal reviewers and external auditors, IT staff, and potential information users will be delivered by a team of trainers managed by the PMU with the assistance of external consultants. Given the potentially high numbers of recipients of information about NPSAS, a "train the trainer" approach is very likely to be adopted so that the dissemination of information can reach all levels of government within the prescribed time frames and budgets. It is also important that guidance is given to users of the new financial information so that they can take full advantage of it in their role as decision-makers.

Tactical recruitment of new graduates in accounting should also be budgeted for and carried out by objective need foreseen by the training and recruitment plan.

2.1.6 End Point of Phase 1

Fifteen NPSAS should have been made available by budget organizations, STFs, and local government though only some may be fully implemented, and one may be withdrawn. The IPSAS conceptual framework will also be an authority for these entities. New reporting formats, including cash flow and budget variance statements, should also be available for publication. Interested parties—including the senior accountants at budget organizations who must consolidate the financial results of several entities within their institutional group—will have a more developed awareness of best practice consolidation rules following their training in the principles of IPSAS 35.

In preparation for phase 2, an inventory of SOEs, identifying those in the government sector and public corporations, would have been carried out.

2.2 Phase 2 Actions

Table 3: Phase 2 Actions

Start Point of the Phase	Standards and Regulatory Framework Actions	Reporting, Accounting, COA, and IT Actions	Training and Other Actions	End Point of the Phase
Beginning of 2022	2022–2023			End of 2023
• Fifteen NPSAS are developed and mainly, if not entirely, applied by budget organizations and STFs • PMU and external consultants continue to work together • M&E / help desk provides satisfactory support to preparers of NPSAS financial statements	• Ten new NPSAS are adapted to IPSAS (and accounting policies within NAS), two are taken from phase 1 • Consolidation boundary may be expanded to include not-for-profit SOEs, subject to government approval • Consolidation rules based on IPSAS 35 are further tested for compliance within a wider consolidation boundary • Regulatory changes enable new accounting and reporting requirements	• Financial reports of entities in the scope of NPSAS for 2021 and 2022 are broadly in line with IPSAS • The practice of recognizing and measuring debt assets and liabilities is incorporated in the financial statements • Necessary changes to IT systems and COA are specified and coded to enable amended accounting and reporting requirements	• Further NPSAS awareness-raising events on the new standards are held • NPSAS training materials for MOF officials, auditors, and accountants in the reporting entities are developed and disseminated • PMU and M&E functions continue to operate • E-learning training materials made available to practitioners and auditors • Continue selective recruitment	• A total of 25 NPSAS are developed and available for use and either withdrawn, implemented, or substantially implemented • New reporting formats, including all government sector debt data, are made available to PFM experts and, to some extent, the public • Entities within the scope of NPSAS can consolidate financial results in line with IPSAS 35

COA = chart of accounts, IPSAS = International Public Sector Accounting Standards, IT = information technology, M&E = monitoring and evaluation, MOF = Ministry of Finance, NAS = national accounting standards, NPSAS = National Public Sector Accounting Standards, PFM = public financial management, PMU = Project Management Unit, SOEs = state-owned enterprises, STF = state targeted fund.

Source: Consultan’ts analysis.

2.2.1 Starting Point of Phase 2

By the beginning of phase 2, most of the 15 NPSAS developed by the end of phase 1 will be applied by budget organizations and STFs. The PMU and external consultants will continue to work together and prepare to begin the work necessary for the second phase of NPSAS development. However, there may be a few areas, such as property, plant, and equipment, where implementation will not be complete until phase 2 (see section 4 for details). The monitoring and evaluation (M&E) function at the MOF and a remote help-desk service should provide satisfactory support to those who prepare NPSAS-compliant financial statements.

2.2.2 Standards and Regulatory Framework

Phase 2 will see the beginning of adopting a further 10 new NPSAS according to a phased plan for developing national public sector standards identifying those most important for Uzbekistan. Two NPSAS first developed in phase 1 will be redrafted based on revised IPSAS. Fair value and impairment concepts will be embedded in the standards and methodologies.

Subject to government approval, the scope of NPSAS will be extended to include the not-for-profit SOEs identified by the inventory that should be completed by the end of phase 1. This would bring the coverage in line with the IMF's GFS reporting framework allowing IPSAS 22 with consolidated reports to be produced in phase 3.

Alternatively, if the SOEs within the government sector are required to continue reporting based on IFRS, in accordance with NAS based on IFRS, bringing them under the scope of NPSAS would not be feasible. As noted above, to comply with IPSAS, only commercial SOEs with a profit motive should use IFRS as their accounting and reporting framework. If noncommercial SOEs are still required to report under NAS during the phase, the MOF should continue to align the relevant accounting policies in new NPSAS standards with those contained in NAS standards to minimize the adjustments required to consolidate the financial reports of the general government sector (GGS).

Since this will be the second and subsequent year of NPSAS reporting, comparative figures can be incorporated within the financial reports.

2.2.3 Reporting and Accounting Actions

During phase 2, the financial reports of entities in the scope of NPSAS for the financial years 2021 and 2022 are to be produced by the reports and presentation formats contained in IPSAS. The practice of recognizing and measuring government debt assets and liabilities will be expanded so that by the end of phase 2, government debt will be as fully reflected as possible in the consolidated balance sheet for the government sector.

2.2.4 Chart of Accounts and Information Technology Systems Actions

As with phase 1, all amendments to IT systems and the UCOA made necessary by changes in the scope and structure of financial reports will be specified and coded to enable the new accounting and reporting requirements.

2.2.5 Training and Other Actions

During phase 2, further NPSAS awareness-raising and training events on the new standards will be held in central and regional locations according to an overall training plan. Regional training will be provided by trainers engaged in phase 1 dissemination. Revised NPSAS training materials will be developed and disseminated for MOF officials, auditors, financial statement reviewers, and senior accountants in the reporting entities. Further guidance will be given on using the new-style financial reports for decision-making purposes, including a greater level of disclosure than in phase 1.

Selective recruitment of accounting graduates or recently qualified accountants should be carried out alongside training of existing staff. Where possible, training materials are to be transmitted digitally using web-based platforms. E-learning training courses and online user discussion forums can enable self-learning and self-help communities to deepen user understanding of how to apply the new NPSAS.

The PMU and M&E functions set up at the beginning of the implementation will continue to operate during phase 2, providing project management, supporting communication of activities to the users, and reviewing implementation progress to gauge the effectiveness of NPSAS training and dissemination.

2.2.6 End Point of Phase 2

By the end of phase 2, a total of at least 25 NPSAS should have been developed. The scope of the entities preparing NPSAS financial statements would have expanded to include not-for-profit SOEs by then. New reporting formats recognizing and measuring all government sector debt could be available to PFM specialists in the country and, to a more limited extent, to the public.

Following the support received by the MOF in applying the NPSAS based on IPSAS 35, including training and the automation of processes to identify and eliminate inter-entity balances, entities within the scope of NPSAS should be able to consolidate financial results according to best practices.

Upon completion of this phase, an interim review of progress should be carried out to determine whether it is necessary to reschedule the remaining phases of the IPSAS Implementation Road Map. This could be required if, for example, some standards planned to commence during phase 2 were not started on time and needed to be deferred to phase 3. This may, in turn, lead to a deferral of the start date of the development of standards scheduled for phase 3, and the consequence of that could be that the planned duration of phase 3 would be formally extended in the revised implementation plan.

2.3 Phase 3 Actions

Table 4: Phase 3 Actions

Start Point of the Phase	Standards and Regulatory Framework Actions	Reporting, Accounting, COA, and IT Actions	Training and Other Actions	End Point of the Phase
		2024–2025		
Beginning of 2024	⟵	⟶		**End of 2025**
• Twenty-five NPSAS are mostly, if not fully, applied by budget organizations and STFs • Some SOEs may be reporting under NPSAS • PMU and M&E/help desk continue to support users	• Final NPSAS are adapted to remaining IPSAS, considering NAS accounting policies • Consolidation boundary may be expanded to include public corporations, subject to government approval. If not, cross-framework consolidation will be practiced • Compliance with consolidation rules continues to be monitored • Regulatory changes to enable new accounting and reporting requirements are made	• Financial reports of entities in the scope of NPSAS for 2023 and 2024 are in line with IPSAS • The practice of recognizing and measuring debt assets and liabilities is refined • Contingent liabilities/third-party payments are also reflected in the accounting systems • Necessary changes to IT systems and COA are implemented to enable amended accounting and reporting needs	• Further NPSAS awareness-raising events on the new standards are held • NPSAS training materials for MOF officials, auditors, and accountants in the reporting entities are developed and disseminated • PMU and M&E functions continue to operate • E-learning training materials made available to practitioners and auditors • Revise training needs analysis and training and recruitment plan	• NPSAS are fully developed and available for use in line with the current suite of IPSASs • New reporting formats, including contingent liabilities, third-party payments, and all government sector debt are presented openly • The MOF has the experience to manage the next part of the transition to full IPSAS if the government approves the switch from NAS for public sector entities

COA = chart of accounts, IPSAS = International Public Sector Accounting Standards, IT = information technology, M&E = monitoring and evaluation, MOF = Ministry of Finance, NAS = national accounting standards, NPSAS = National Public Sector Accounting Standards, PMU = Project Management Unit, SOEs = state-owned enterprises, STF = state targeted fund.

Source: Consultant's analysis.

2.3.1 Starting Point of Phase 3

By the beginning of phase 3, the development of 25 NPSAS should have been started and applied by budget organizations, STFs, and not-for-profit SOEs. Consolidated financial statements are to be produced in line with the NPSAS based on IPSAS 35, whose development began in phase 2.

At the end of phase 2, a decision could be made based on experience so far to extend the duration of phase 3 beyond the 2 years initially envisaged. The phase must last long enough to enable the application of all NPSASs before transitioning to phase 4.

The PMU and external consultants must be ready to continue their collaboration during this important phase of NPSAS development. The M&E Unit and the help-desk service should continue providing constructive feedback to those who prepare NPSAS-compliant financial statements.

2.3.2 Standards and Regulatory Framework

This phase will involve the adoption of all remaining IPSASs in place at the time.[5] In addition, fiscal risk will be identified in a register of government contingent liabilities and third-party payments. This information will be incorporated into the financial reports. Public financial reporting will also include information about external and other assistance. NAS accounting policies will be considered in drafting NPSASs to facilitate easier consolidation of financial results across the public sector.

During phase 3, the consolidation boundary of entities reporting under NPSAS may expand to include public corporations depending on the government's relevant policy decisions. If an SOE is controlled by another entity controlled by the government, both entities are classified in either the government or the public corporation sectors using the criteria defined by GFS and IPSAS. The MOF should verify continued compliance with IPSAS 35 rules during phase 3.

2.3.3 Chart of Accounts and Information Technology Systems Actions

During this phase, these fundamental improvements to accounting systems and procedures may be required:

(i) Implementing an integrated budget classification and COA based on the GFS 2014 Annex 4 structure, also amended to meet the NPSAS requirements.

(ii) Specifying a new Integrated Financial Management Information System (IFMIS) to integrate within a single system the functions of the Information System for Public Financial Management (ISPFM) and Uzbekistan Automated System for Budget Organizations (UZASBO) systems. Each system holds its own database of transactions, meaning that transactions involving cash flows are recorded in both systems. However, a fundamental principle of designing relational databases is that each transaction is entered only once (with double entries established using the ledgers, which are tables within the system).

2.3.4 Training and Other Actions

During phase 3, further awareness-raising and training events will be held in central and regional locations. NPSAS training materials relating to the remaining standards will be developed for and disseminated to MOF officials, auditors, and senior accountants in the reporting entities, preferably using web-based platforms but also involving printed publications. Again, guidance will be given to decision-makers on how to make the best use of this new information.

E-learning training courses will be developed for the new NPSAS, and online user communities will be supported and encouraged to debate the technical issues arising from the latest standards.

[5] It is very likely that, given the nature of IPSAS, new standards will have been added to the current suite and potentially some removed, so it is not possible at this stage to definitively state how many IPSASs will be in place in 2024 and 2025.

The scope of training should include special refresher workshops on financial consolidation practice relating to entities within the scope of NPSAS and, if necessary, specific instruction on consolidating the results of entities reporting under NPSAS, NAS, and IFRS. Training activities and materials will also cover any changes to the UCOA and reporting formats.

Before the end of the phase, a revised training (and recruitment) needs analysis should be carried out by the MOF Training Centre, and an updated training plan should be formulated. The training needs analysis should identify any training or recruitment gaps potentially preventing Uzbekistan from moving to phase 4 of the Implementation Road Map. The new training and recruitment plan should indicate how to close those gaps.

2.3.5 End Point of Phase 3

By the end of this phase, all but one of the IPSASs will have been adapted to the NPSAS; IPSAS 33 will be the only remaining standard, to be adopted for the first time. However, as explained above, this should always be used as a benchmark because of its valuable guidance on phasing the implementation of accruals-based standards.

The updated formats of the NPSAS financial statements, including disclosure notes, should present balances for contingent liabilities, third-party payments, and all government sector debt accurately and transparently. Indeed, there will be extensive disclosures in all areas covered by the NPSAS. All required consolidation processes will have been implemented and verified as functional.

By the end of Phase 3, the MOF will have the experience and capability to manage the next stage of the transition toward full IPSAS.

2.4 Phase 4 Actions

Table 5: Phase 4 Actions

Start Point of the Phase	Standards and Regulatory Framework Actions	Reporting, Accounting, COA, and IT Actions	Training and Other Actions	End Point of the Phase
		2026–2030		
Beginning of 2026	⟷			**End of 2030**
• All NPSAS are applied by budget organizations and STFs • Some SOEs may be reporting under NPSAS • PMU and M&E / help desk continue to support users	• A plan for introducing all IPSAS standards in line with IPSAS 33 (first-time application) is drafted • NPSAS are entirely superseded by IPSAS • The IPSAS consolidation boundary includes almost all public sector entities (if the government agrees) • IPSAS entities are internally consolidated, and IFRS entities are added separately to produce whole-of-public-sector accounts • Regulatory changes are made to enable all technical requirements	• All financial reports of entities in the scope of IPSAS are fully compliant with the relevant standards • The qualities of useful financial information in the IPSAS conceptual framework are restated • A full IFMIS is implemented to support IPSAS consolidated financial reporting	• IPSAS training materials for MOF officials, auditors, and accountants in the reporting entities are developed and disseminated • PMU and M&E functions continue to operate • E-learning training materials are made available to practitioners and auditors • Verification of internalized knowledge of IPSAS is continually undertaken	• All extant IPSAS have been adopted and are in use by the in-scope reporting entities • The principles and guidelines of IPSAS are integrated into accounting and reporting practices

COA = chart of accounts, IPSAS = International Public Sector Accounting Standards, IFMIS = integrated financial management information system, IFRS = international financial reporting standards, IT = information technology, M&E = monitoring and evaluation, MOF = Ministry of Finance, NPSAS = National Public Sector Accounting Standards, PMU = Project Management Unit, SOEs = state-owned enterprises, STF = state targeted fund.

Source: Consultant's analysis.

2.4.1 The Period of Transition to Full International Public Sector Accounting Standards

During the first three phases, the NPSASs developed and disseminated by the MOF—assisted by national and international experts—should have been progressively adapted to IPSAS, while national variants of international standards remain. These first three phases have been designed to align Uzbekistan's public sector financial reports more closely with the full extent of IPSAS reporting requirements. Adopting IPSASs must lead to their principles and rules becoming embedded in Uzbekistan's accounting and reporting practice.

Reaching the beginning of phase 4 is feasible from a technical point of view, provided the MOF receives sufficient practical support up to that point, but moving to a full IPSAS implementation is contingent on the country's PFM policies.

Whatever decision is taken about the scope of IPSASs, it is believed that a new IFMIS (specified in the road map as an activity for phase 3) will need to be acquired and implemented during phase 4 to underpin sound public sector financial reporting in Uzbekistan. International experience suggests this is likely to be a substantial challenge.

3 OBJECTIVES AND STATUS OF THE PROJECT

3.1 Purpose of the Assignment

The objective of the technical assistance assignment financed by ADB is to develop an IPSAS Implementation Road Map for the MOF of Uzbekistan and provide advisory and methodological assistance to the MOF until the formal adoption of the road map.

The implementation in Uzbekistan of financial reporting standards based on IPSAS will enable the following:

(i) enhanced transparency and governance of public spending and revenues;

(ii) a better understanding of the country's financial performance;

(iii) greater accountability to make informed decisions about resource utilization; and

(iv) improved financial information to support better financial governance, asset management, and decision-making.

3.2 Current Status of Public Financial Management in Uzbekistan

3.2.1 Public Financial Management Strategic Plan

The PFM Reform Action Plan 2007–2018 for Uzbekistan predicted that new procedures, classification structures, and computerized accounting systems to strengthen centralized treasury management would become operational during the plan period. To support these important changes, the Department for Methodology and Introduction of Treasury Execution for the State Budget was established in the MOF. The PFM Reform Action Plan also scheduled the introduction of compliance with IPSAS and the Government Finance Statistics Manual by 2018.

Many planned enhancements to the treasury function have been implemented to improve control over cash movements and balances. However, developing a new framework for financial reporting has been carried forward beyond the end of the 2007–2018 PFM Reform Plan. The current ADB-funded project began its collaboration with the MOF in 2018, by confirming the actions required to implement IPSAS or IPSAS-based financial reporting standards.

By the start of this project, 12 national budget standards based on IPSAS have been confirmed by legislation for implementation during 2020. However, some revision to phase 1 of standards to be implemented is necessary due to unforeseen changes to the IPSAS framework (see section 3.2.2).

The MOF's Action Plan for the Harmonization of Budget Accounting with IPSAS had initially envisaged that the 12 standards would be effective from 1 January 2019. Still, implementation has been put back 12 months. Nevertheless, the creation and testing of the UCOA to enable the sharing of accounting data by the Treasury and financial reporting system has been largely completed. The ministry's Action Plan also anticipated that its staff would become involved in disseminating the new standards to practitioners and revising relevant legislative instruments during 2019–2020.

3.2.2 Budgetary and Financial Reporting

The PFM Reform Action Plan 2007–2018 for Uzbekistan emphasized the urgent need for

(i) closer alignment of cash and accrual basis accounting;

(ii) management of Uzbekistan Sum-denominated debt and contingent liabilities;

(iii) expansion of the scope of budget execution reporting (e.g., to include all STFs, extra-budgetary funds, and program budgeting); and

(iv) the adoption of uniform financial reporting standards for enhanced control and efficiency.

All the above have an important bearing on accurately representing public entities' financial positions, which may then be aggregated into the GGS or the public sector (the government sector plus state-controlled commercial entities).

For completeness, however, the scope of an accrual IPSAS implementation, in addition to the above four items emphasized by the PFM Reform Plan, should also feature the following:

(i) a clear statement of intent by the government to consolidate (or a clear decision not to consolidate) accrual financial information into reports for the GGS or, preferably, the entire public sector, to obtain a "whole-of-sector" view of state finances;

(ii) all foreign currency-denominated transactions (including receipts, payments, assets, and liabilities) belonging to budget organizations and all other public entities regardless of whether they pass through the treasury single account, that is, including accrual information;

(iii) debt assets and liabilities, as well as contingent liabilities arising in connection with binding loan agreements rather than only debt-related cash movements;

(iv) any other tangible assets and liabilities arising, including those relating to payments to third parties;

(v) specific forms of reporting defined by IPSAS, including much greater narrative disclosure of relevant information in the financial statements themselves; and

(vi) the qualitative characteristics of financial information central to the IPSAS philosophy.

3.2.3 *Government's International Public Sector Accounting Standards Reform Strategy*

As part of implementing the government's PFM Reform Strategy 2007–2018, 12 NPSASs based on IPSAS have been scheduled for imminent introduction, as stated in section 3.2.2 and listed in Table 6.

Table 6: National Public Sector Accounting Standards for Adoption in the First Phase of the International Public Sector Accounting Standards Implementation

NPSAS (No. / Title)		Equivalent IPSAS (No. / Title)		Comments
1	Accounting policies	3	Accounting policies, changes in accounting estimates, and errors	NPSAS 1 expands on the principles of accounting in Uzbekistan but excludes accounting estimates and errors
2	Chart of accounts	No equivalent IPSAS exists		See comments below
3	Financial reports	1	Presentation of financial statements	See comments below
		24	Presentation of budget information in financial statements	
4	Exchange rates	4	The effects of changes in foreign exchange rates	These NPSAS have not been reviewed in detail but appear to be broadly consistent with IPSAS though much shorter, with far fewer disclosures and options or consideration of special circumstances
5	Agriculture	27	Agriculture	
6	Leases	13	Leases (soon to be updated based on Exposure Draft 64)	
7	Inventories	12	Inventories	
8	Property, plant, and equipment	17	Property, plant, and equipment	
9	Intangible assets	31	Intangible assets	
10	Revenue from exchange transactions	9	Revenue from exchange transactions (possibly impacted by changes to IPSAS 9 in the near future)	
11	Borrowing costs	5	Borrowing costs	
12	Construction costs	11	Construction contracts	The IPSAS Board may eliminate IPSAS 11 soon

IPSAS = International Public Sector Accounting Standards, NPSAS = National Public Sector Accounting Standards.
Source: Consultant's analysis.

The introduction of these 12 NPSASs is a significant step forward. Their implementation will result in enhanced financial reporting by the government. However, implementers of NPSAS should be aware that, as adoptions of IPSAS financial reporting standards, NAS

(i) must be constantly reviewed to ensure consistency with IPSAS, which are themselves frequently updated;

(ii) are usually different, either intentionally or accidentally, from IPSAS and cannot be described as entirely consistent with IPSAS; and

(iii) will need to be made as consistent as possible with NAS based on IFRS to enable the consolidation of financial reports produced by the budget sector, all SOEs, and any other commercial public sector organizations.

Nevertheless, NPSAS allows Uzbekistan to progressively implement standards based on IPSAS following national priorities. This is the approach adopted by the government. Based on these standards, during 2020, it was planned to develop and publish NPSAS financial reports for the consolidated budget for the financial year 2019.[6] However, a detailed review of the current status of the NPSASs framework suggests that some modifications may be needed (section 4).

To achieve this outcome, several further important reforms have already been initiated:

(i) A new UCOA has been developed that will be combined in the Treasury system (ISPFM) and budget organizations' financial reporting system (UZASBO) to enable reporting in accordance with NPSAS 3.

(ii) ISPFM and UZASBO will be upgraded to enable the same new COA to be applied to them both and for the automated consolidation of information.

The analysis in the following section considers the importance of phasing the implementation of the NPSAS logically and realistically. It then considers the importance of developing the UCOA further to provide a solid data platform on which to build financial reports in the future.

6 The original plan was to introduce the standards and report against them a year earlier than is now intended.

4 IMPLEMENTATION PHASING, CLOSING EXISTING GAPS, AND DEVELOPMENT OF THE CHART OF ACCOUNTS

4.1 Implementation Phasing and Closing Existing Gaps

4.1.1 *The Phasing of the First Batch of 12 National Public Sector Accounting Standards*

In the first batch, a total of 12 NPSASs have been developed, as shown in Table 7. These have been published, and high-level training is intended, though no detailed training plans have yet been drawn up, and training materials on NPSAS are only partially developed. Experience from other countries reveals that a realistic phasing of the implementation of new accrual basis standards is key to a successful outcome. Beginning with 12 standards is an ambitious target. It is one thing to develop standards defining what should be reported and how, but another to practically implement them. Some standards will likely take several years to implement. Only detailed working on the data and information required to comply with the new standards will reveal the gaps.

It is also probable that some standards will continue to evolve over the life cycle of the implementation period. A good example concerns IPSAS 35, consolidated financial statements. The most logical way of implementing this standard for the first time is to progressively widen the boundaries of those entities consolidated over time, as suggested in this road map (see section 5). This could start with, for example, the central government, then add other entities covered by the GGS and, ultimately, include all commercial SOEs (subject to political approval) to cover the whole public sector. This process will likely take many years and cover multiple phases of the proposed road map as its scope expands.

It is also likely that those standards currently stated for the initial phase will not all be implemented until phase 2 and beyond. A good example relates to NPSAS 8, which is based on IPSAS 17, property, plant, and equipment. Discussions with counterparts reveal some potentially significant challenges regarding using appropriate valuations for the assets involved. This issue may take some time to overcome. Similarly, depreciation costs will need to be allocated into specific classification categories; currently, they are aggregated into one total figure. It may also take time to address this historical legacy problem. Therefore, the requirements of NPSAS 8 will only be possible until after phase 1 of the road map.

In some examples of standards currently included in the first phase—the IPSAS, on which the NPSAS is based—is likely to be superseded soon. For example, it is known that at least one IPSAS mapping to the 12 standards developed is likely to be withdrawn in the near future, while two others are to be extensively revised. In such instances, there may be merit in deferring the implementation of the proposed NPSAS until a new IPSAS is issued to manage the workload more efficiently and prevent abortive work.

Detailed proposals, including suggested amendments to the implementation phasing, and the likely implementation timescales for each NPSAS included in phase 1, and a possible phasing for the remaining NPSAS are shown in Tables 7 and 8. The implementation of some of the standards is likely to straddle several phases.

Table 7: Proposed Implementation Phasing for National Public Sector Accounting Standards Already Developed

NPSAS	Title	Likely Implementation Period			
		Phase 1	Phase 2	Phase 3	Phase 4
1	Accounting policies	✓			
2	Chart of accounts	✓	✓	✓	
3	Financial reports	✓	✓	✓	✓
4	Exchange rates	✓			
5	Agriculture	✓	✓		
6	Leases	(✓)	✓	✓	
7	Inventories	✓	✓		
8	Property, plant, and equipment	✓	✓		
9	Intangible assets	✓	✓		
10	Revenue from exchange transactions	(✓)	✓		
11	Borrowing costs	✓			
12	Construction costs	(✓)			

NPSAS = National Public Sector Accounting Standards, (✓) = standard is drafted, but implementation may be deferred until a later phase.

Source: Consultant's analysis.

More detailed comments on the NPSAS already developed are grouped thematically below.

- **Longer implementation periods for some NPSAS than a single phase**: Some NPSAS may start to be implemented in phase 1 but may not be finished until phase 2 or beyond. These include agriculture (NPSAS 5); inventories (NPSAS 7); property, plant, and equipment (NPSAS 8); and intangible assets (NPSAS 9), where various complexities relating to the collection of appropriate data may arise. The perception that there are likely to be extended timescales for full implementation of these arises partly from discussions with counterparts and partly from the experience of other countries in implementing accruals-based standards in these areas.

  The scope of the specific content of financial reports (NPSAS 3), which is a high-level standard on the structure of financial statements, is likely to evolve over the entire implementation timescale as new elements are progressively added over time. The COA revision (as per NPSAS 2, there is no equivalent IPSAS) is likely to evolve as other standards are developed, and this has been reflected in the likely phasing shown in Table 7.

- **Deferral of implementing some standards**: It is proposed that implementing three of the NPSASs already developed are deferred until phase 2. There are compelling reasons for this. The overall approach for the development of NPSAS in Uzbekistan is that they will link to an equivalent IPSAS, and in the three cases above, the IPSASs to which the NPSAS are linked are currently under review by the International Public Sector Accounting Standards Board (IPSASB). These IPSASs are likely to change significantly soon. To avoid abortive work, which would be the case if NPSASs were amended considerably after they have been issued, it is proposed that the implementation of NPSAS 6 and NPSAS 10 be delayed to phase 2, by which time new IPSAS standards on leasing and revenue recognition, respectively, should be in place. It is possible that IPSAS 11 on construction contracts to which NPSAS 12 is linked will be eliminated in future IPSAS revisions, so this NPSAS may never become operational as it is likely to be replaced by new revenue recognition guidance included in other standards.

4.1.2 Closing Gaps Arising from the First Batch of 12 National Public Sector Accounting Standards

The first 12 NPSASs developed have been compared to the equivalent IPSAS (where it exists), and resultant gaps have been identified. **The following analysis is consistent with that presented in greater detail in the gap analysis accompanying this road map**. Also, our proposals for addressing misalignments between the NPSAS developed and the relevant IPSAS during phase 1 are set out.

NPSAS 1

Gap Identified: NPSAS 1 needs to be more active on accounting errors and estimates and omits much information on disclosing first-time adoption or voluntary changes in accounting policies. Moreover, whereas IPSAS 3 indicates that changes in accounting policies should be driven by the need to provide more relevant information about the effects of transactions on the entity's financial position, the relevant paragraph in NPSAS mentions that accounting policies should only be changed following amendments to the legislation regulating the budget, as well as the reorganization of the budget organization.

NPSAS 1 refers to some principles of accounting that use similar terminology to that found in IPSAS 1. However, there needs to be more due emphasis on the qualitative characteristics of information in financial statements that make it helpful to users. The four principal qualitative characteristics defined by IPSAS are understandability, relevance, reliability, and comparability. Although NPSAS do not claim to be IPSAS standards, nevertheless, it is a prerequisite that they agree with the fundamental characteristics of IPSAS.

Proposed Measure to Close Gap: Draft-relevant missing elements of IPSAS 3 in a suitable format for inclusion in a revised version of NPSAS 1.

The MOF should adopt the IPSAS conceptual framework as the essential frame of reference for all NPSASs that it issues. Current and future versions of NPSAS should, as far as possible, balance the qualitative aspects of financial reporting under IPSAS with the legal context in Uzbekistan. The IPSAS conceptual framework also enables users to develop accounting policies should they come across specific issues that are not dealt with by an existing standard.

NPSAS 2

Gap Identified: NPSAS 2 has no equivalent IPSAS.

In the new COA proposed by NPSAS 2, some items are shown in a section called off-balance sheet notes, which includes lines for, among other things, bad debt write-offs and some types of inventory. The use of such accounts could indicate an intention to reduce the visibility of such transactions and not to reflect their actual substance.

Proposed Measure to Close Gap: IPSAS is separate from the question of the COA. This anomaly does no harm to the functioning of NPSAS and so may remain in place.

It would be better to use supplementary recording mechanisms outside of the COA to capture the necessary details of such items while still representing the substance of all transactions within the accounting system in use.

NPSAS 3

Gap Identified: NPSAS 3 needs to be updated to bring in guidance on the cash flow statement and the statement of comparison of budget to actual.

The template financial reports in NPSAS 3 need guidance on, or even space in which to append, disclosure notes. There is a noticeable absence of disclosure notes in the current suite of budget execution reports when compared to international examples of financial statements based on IPSAS.

The implementation guidance in NPSAS 3 mainly describes the structure of the financial reports but provides relatively little additional information that could help practitioners apply the new standards accurately.

Proposed Measure to Close Gap: The relevant guidance, including formats of the cash flow statement and the statement of comparison of budget to actual should be added to NPSAS 3.

The formats of reports originally included in NPSAS 3 should be amended in line with IPSAS, including appropriate provision for disclosure notes.

NPSAS 3 should be expanded to provide more implementation guidance to practitioners and explain how users of the financial reports could be assisted to understand better the reporting entity's financial position or cash flows.

NPSAS 6

Gap Identified: NPSAS 6 provides relatively little implementation guidance on calculating lease payments compared to IPSAS 13.

Proposed Measure to Clo se Gap: IPSAS 13, on which NPSAS 6 is based, may change significantly soon; therefore, NPSAS 6 will probably need to be updated in any event.

NPSAS 7

Gap Identified: NPSAS 7 suggests that inventories from non-exchange transactions should be valued at their purchase price but, by definition, prices do not apply to such transactions; instead, inventories acquired in this way must be measured at their estimated market value as at the date of acquisition.

NPSAS 7 mistakenly calls the average weighted valuation method of measuring the cost of inventory "fair value."

Proposed Measure to Close Gap: Any inaccuracies in the current drafting of NPSAS 7 should be addressed during 2020.

NPSAS 8

Gap Identified: The measurement of asset values in NPSAS 8 is restricted to historical cost modified by periodic revaluations, whereas IPSAS 17 permits using fair value as a measurement model. Fair value is more complicated to implement, but it upholds the principle of fair representation better than the modified historical cost in most situations where it could be used.

Proposed Measure to Close Gap: As stated elsewhere in this road map and confirmed by the proposed scheduling of NPSAS 8 in Table 7 and of the NPSAS based on IPSAS 21 and IPSAS 26 (Table 3), the concepts of fair value and impairment will be embedded in the standards and accounting methodologies over phases 1 and 2 to allow sufficient time for them to be fully grasped by practitioners.

NPSAS 11

Gap Identified: NPSAS 11 does not mention the expensing of borrowing costs as the default treatment or refer to management judgment in deciding how to measure the cost of borrowing when different sources of financing are potentially involved.

Proposed Measure to Close Gap: Any inaccuracies in the current drafting of NPSAS 11 should be addressed during 2020.

NPSAS 12

Gap Identified: NPSAS 12 does not explicitly state that when the outcome of a construction contract cannot be estimated reliably, revenue should be recognized to the extent of contract costs incurred that are likely to be recoverable. Instead, it recommends measuring revenue as the costs incurred up to that point.

There are some current accruals-based practices that need to be entirely consistent with IPSAS and should ideally be brought into line. These include the following:

(i) There is no capitalization threshold in place for fixed assets.

(ii) While items are annually reviewed to see where there is an asset that should be written off, there may be some time delay before the write-off takes place.

(iii) The current process of revaluing assets using an index at the start of the year is out of sync with international practice.

Proposed Measure to Close Gap: IPSAS 11, on which NPSAS 12 is based, may change significantly and possibly even be eliminated soon. If so, the revenue recognition arising from construction contracts will be governed by standards dedicated to this subject, and both IPSAS 11 and NPSAS 12 will become redundant.

Although IPSAS does not require this, it is regularly found internationally. A capitalization threshold prescribes that, even if an item has all the essential characteristics of a non-current asset, it will not be treated as such because it is of too low a value.

IPSAS 17, which is the IPSAS equivalent of NPSAS 8, requires annual impairment reviews to see if assets are currently overvalued. IPSAS 21, linked to IPSAS 17, requires that a provision be made as soon as it appears probable (i.e., greater than 50% probability) that it will be written off at some stage in the future. If revaluation is used, then it should be done at the end of the financial year. Further, it appears that any gains recognized on revaluation are debited to a fixed asset account code, and the credit is posted to depreciation (which is not correct, this side of the entry should go to a revaluation reserve).

4.1.3 *The Phasing of Future National Public Sector Accounting Standards*

Moving on to the remaining current "live" IPSAS for which no NPSAS has yet been developed, Table 8 shows a suggested implementation phasing for these. In a few cases, it is proposed that some be brought forward to phase 1. It is appreciated that it is quite late in the day to introduce new elements to phase 1, but early translation and implementation planning for these is likely to be beneficial in the longer run. These standards are what might be called overarching high-level standards, which provide an essential foundation for the full development of IPSAS/NPSAS.

Table 8: Proposed Implementation Phasing for Remaining International Public Sector Accounting Standards

IPSAS	Title	Proposed Phasing			
		Phase 1	Phase 2	Phase 3	Phase 4
IPSAS 2	Cash flow statements	✓			
IPSAS 10	Financial reporting in hyperinflationary economies			✓	
IPSAS 14	Events after the reporting date			✓	
IPSAS 16	Investment property			✓	
IPSAS 18	Segment reporting			✓	
IPSAS 19	Provisions, contingent liabilities, and contingent assets		✓	✓	
IPSAS 20	Related party disclosures			✓	
IPSAS 21	Impairment of non-cash-generating assets		✓		
IPSAS 22	Disclosure of financial information about the general government sector		✓		
IPSAS 23	Revenue from non-exchange transactions (taxes and transfers)		✓	✓	
IPSAS 24	Presentation of budget information in financial statements	✓			
IPSAS 26	Impairment of cash-generating assets		✓		
IPSAS 28	Financial instruments: presentation			✓	
IPSAS 30	Financial instruments: disclosures			✓	
IPSAS 32	Service concession arrangements: grantor		✓		
IPSAS 33	First-time adoption of accrual basis International Public Sector Accounting Standards	[✓]	[✓]	[✓]	✓
IPSAS 34	Separate financial statements			✓	
IPSAS 35	Consolidated financial statements	✓	✓	✓	✓
IPSAS 36	Investments in associates and joint ventures			✓	
IPSAS 37	Joint arrangements			✓	
IPSAS 38	Disclosure of interests in other entities		✓		
IPSAS 39	Employee benefits		✓	✓	
IPSAS 40	Public sector combinations			✓	
IPSAS 41	Financial instruments		✓	✓	
IPSAS 42	Social benefits		✓		

IPSAS = International Public Sector Accounting Standards, [✓] = IPSAS 33 may be consulted as a guide to implementing National Public Sector Accounting Standards incrementally before it is used as the standard for first-time adoption of the full IPSAS framework.

Source: Consultant's analysis.

These remaining standards are identified in Table 9, after which commentaries explain the rationale behind these proposals.

Table 9: Four-Phased Implementation Plan for National Public Sector Accounting Standards

NPSAS	Title	Phase in Which the NPSAS Originates			
		Phase 1	Phase 2	Phase 3	Phase 4
1	Accounting policies	✓			
2	Chart of accounts	✓			
3	Financial reports	✓			
4	Exchange rates	✓			
5	Agriculture	✓			
6	Leases	(✓)			
7	Inventories	✓			
8	Property, plant, and equipment	✓			
9	Intangible assets	✓			
10	Revenue from exchange transactions	(✓)			
11	Borrowing costs	✓			
12	Construction costs	(✓)			
13	Addition to NPSAS 3 based on IPSAS 2	✓			
14	New NPSAS based on IPSAS 24	✓			
15	New NPSAS based on IPSAS 35	✓			
16	New NPSAS based on IPSAS 19		✓		
17	New NPSAS based on IPSAS 21		✓		
18	New NPSAS based on IPSAS 22		✓		
19	New NPSAS based on IPSAS 23		✓		
20	New NPSAS based on IPSAS 26		✓		
21	New NPSAS based on IPSAS 32		✓		
22	New NPSAS based on IPSAS 38		✓		
23	New NPSAS based on IPSAS 39		✓		
24	New NPSAS based on IPSAS 41		✓		
25	New NPSAS based on IPSAS 42		✓		
26	New NPSAS based on IPSAS 10			✓	
27	New NPSAS based on IPSAS 14			✓	
28	New NPSAS based on IPSAS 16			✓	
29	New NPSAS based on IPSAS 18			✓	
30	New NPSAS based on IPSAS 20			✓	
31	New NPSAS based on IPSAS 28			✓	
32	New NPSAS based on IPSAS 30			✓	
33	New NPSAS based on IPSAS 34			✓	
34	New NPSAS based on IPSAS 36			✓	
35	New NPSAS based on IPSAS 37			✓	
36	New NPSAS based on IPSAS 40			✓	
37	New NPSAS based on IPSAS 33				✓
Totals		**15**	**10**	**11**	**1**

IPSAS = International Public Sector Accounting Standards, NPSAS = National Public Sector Accounting Standards, (✓) = standard is drafted, but implementation may be deferred until a later phase.

Source: Consultant's analysis.

Bringing the Start of Some National Public Sector Accounting Standards Forward to Phase 1

- It is proposed that some standards be added to phase 1 due to their high-level significance. Cash flow statements (IPSAS 2) and presentation of budget statements (IPSAS 24) both concern the development of core financial statements and should be introduced alongside NPSAS 3 (financial reports).
- IPSAS 33 (first-time adoption of accrual basis IPSAS) is particularly useful when introducing accruals-based standards, IPSASs, or otherwise, for the first time. It has beneficial guidance on the sequencing of implementation and the interconnected nature of various standards. For this reason, it is proposed that this particular standard be translated and analyzed as soon as possible, as it will help shape the thinking of the authorities when phasing the implementation of the NPSAS.
- IPSAS 35 is also important as it deals with widening the consolidation base for financial statements. As suggested elsewhere in this road map (see section 5), the progressive development of wider consolidation boundaries across the implementation period is a key factor in improving the quality and coverage of the annual financial statements, and IPSAS 35 is important in providing detailed guidance on this.

Selecting National Public Sector Accounting Standards to Start and Be Implemented in Phase 2

- The two impairment standards (IPSAS 21 and IPSAS 26) are essential as they deal with the potential writing-down of asset values whose future economic benefits have been impaired because of obsolescence, damage, etc. In practice, in several countries, such impairments are often overlooked, leading to a potential overstatement of asset values on the balance sheet/ statement of financial position. It is proposed that these important standards be introduced in phase 2, implementing NPSAS 8 on property, plant, and equipment. IPSAS 17, to which NPSAS 8 is linked, makes explicit references to impairment and is logically connected to IPSAS 21 and IPSAS 26.

National Public Sector Accounting Standards Starting in Phase 2 but Continuing into Later Phases

- Financial instruments (IPSAS 28, IPSAS 30, and IPSAS 41) are collectively voluminous standards (IPSAS 41 is over 400 pages long). This reflects that they cover a vast range of issues ranging from fundamental issues such as cash and debt to extremely complex topics such as accounting for derivatives and hedging. Given this wide range of complexity and the sheer size of the standards involved, it is suggested that they should be issued gradually and selectively by the government, starting with those elements of the widest application and finishing with those more complex elements as they appear relevant at the time. An NPSAS based on IPSAS 41 should be introduced in phase 2, and standards based on IPSAS 28 and IPSAS 30 should be implemented in phase 3.
- Some standards are likely to be both important and potentially complex and may take more than one phase to complete. These include revenue from non-exchange transactions (IPSAS 23), which includes, among other things, the requirement to account for tax revenues on an accruals rather than a cash basis; consolidated financial statements (IPSAS 35); provisions, contingent liabilities, and contingent assets (IPSAS 19); financial instruments (IPSAS 41); and employee benefits (IPSAS 39) that include the requirement to account

for pension provisions on an accrual basis. In other countries, these transactions have proved complex to capture though their effect on the overall financial statements has been highly material.[7]

- While IPSAS 10 on financial reporting in hyperinflationary economies is proposed to be included in phase 3, it is possible—as is the case in many other countries—that it will never be needed given its very explicit linkages to those economies faced with a hyperinflationary economic backdrop. Hyperinflation is broadly defined as when inflation exceeds 50% per month, and with inflation currently running at around 17% per year.[8] In Uzbekistan, this is not a current issue.[9]

4.1.4 Developing Future National Public Sector Accounting Standards

To facilitate the maximum possible alignment of NPSAS in development with the IPSAS financial reporting framework, a checklist has been developed to help drafters of new accounting standards based on IPSAS to include all essential elements in the initial and subsequent drafts of each new NPSAS.

The fundamental principles of any new accounting standard should be based on a conceptual framework, such as the IPSAS conceptual framework, which defines the elements of financial statements and the qualitative characteristics of information in those statements.

To ensure close convergence with the concepts and terminology used in IPSAS, the drafting team is strongly advised to use available official IPSAS sources in Russian and to produce the working draft of the new NPSAS in Russian accordingly.

In addition to reviewing the related IPSAS in each case, at an early stage of the NPSAS drafting process, any accounting policies permitted by the NAS (based on IFRS) in the same subject area should be analyzed. By making the accounting policies as consistent as possible, the chances of successfully consolidating the financial reports of SOEs and budget sector entities prepared under the NPSAS and NAS financial reporting frameworks are commensurately increased.

The process of developing an NPSAS standard includes the following steps:

(i) Assess the purpose and context of the proposed standard.

(ii) Produce the first full draft.

(iii) Conduct an expert review of the draft, including wider consultation.

(iv) Make revision(s) to the draft, based on comments received.

(v) Secure MOF approval of the standard.

(vi) Issue a ministerial order promulgating the standard.

(vii) Maintain or revise the new standard.

---

7 As an example, the Civil Service Pension liability in the UK Whole of Government Accounts for 2017–2018 is nearly £1.9 trillion (approximately $2.3 trillion as of 15 August 2019), over 50% of the country's long-term liabilities.

8 Investopedia. 2019. *What Is Hyperinflation? Causes, Effects, Examples, and How to Prepare.*

9 Kun.UZ. 2019. *Inflation Rate in Uzbekistan Increased by 3% in 2018.*

4.1.5 Summary: Closing the Gaps in the Area of Accounting Standards

Given the gaps identified, several important actions should be implemented to bring the current accounting regime closer to the IPSAS financial reporting framework. These are as follows:

(i) The gaps evident in the NPSAS already declared should be examined and a decision made as to whether it is appropriate to rectify them, either immediately or on a longer-term basis.

(ii) The phasing of introducing the new NPSAS should be reviewed and adjusted. For those standards where the corresponding IPSAS (e.g., leasing, revenue) are under review, the implementation of the NPSAS should be delayed, while some others, such as those involving cash flow statements and the statement of comparison of budget to actual, should be added to the list for early implementation.

(iii) There should be greater emphasis on disclosure of information in the annual financial statements than is currently the case. This will improve transparency (and, in turn, accountability) of the annual financial statements and the financial information contained therein.

(iv) A checklist approach for drafting new NPSAS consistent with IPSAS should be adopted.

(v) A technical committee should be established to help develop standards in the future. In addition to representatives from the MOF, this could include others with the requisite accounting knowledge from a sample of line ministries, SOEs, and from external stakeholders such as accounting academics and representatives of civil society organizations. The committee should be moderate (7–8 people) and be given specific terms of reference outlining its roles and responsibilities.

(vi) Revaluations should be made at the end of the current year and reflected in the current year's financial statements as additions to reserves corresponding with the increase in net asset value. They should not be delayed until the start of the following financial year. Indexations in material asset classes should be checked against current market values to gauge their reliability.

4.1.6 Chart of Accounts for National Public Sector Accounting Standards

The Government Finance Statistics Manual 2014 contains a model COA to meet the requirements of GFS reporting and most, but not all, the requirements for IPSAS reporting. There are challenges in extending the GFS COA to meet IPSAS requirements.[10] However, several countries have produced a hybrid COA that does achieve this, for example, Tajikistan, and others are actively developing such models. In addition, individual countries have individual requirements for analyzing cash flows and transactions through a COA and budget classification structures, for example, organizational analysis, spatial analysis, program analysis, source of funds, or simply for more detailed analysis.

Although IPSAS does not specify a COA, the coding requirements for the general ledger are implicit in the analysis required for IPSAS-compliant reports. For budget organizations in Uzbekistan, NPSAS 2 prescribes part (the first six digits) of a new accrual-based UCOA. When combined with seven-digit codes from the budget classification, the resulting 13-digit coding structure is capable of meeting all

[10] GFS is a statistical reporting framework developed by the IMF and is widely used internationally for statistical reporting purposes.

Figure 3: Combined Chart of Accounts Approach

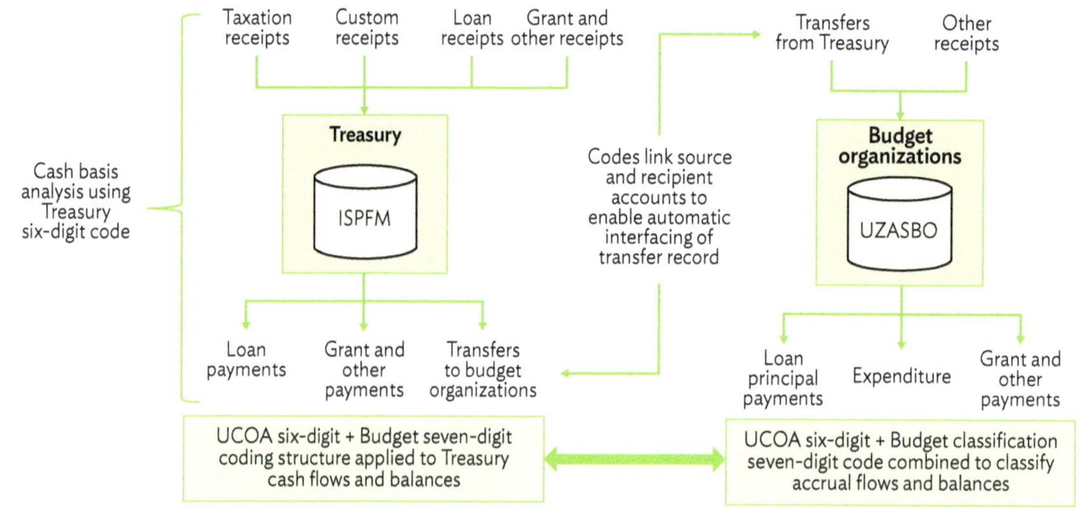

ISPFM = information system for public financial management, UCOA = unified chart of accounts, UZASBO = Uzbekistan Automated System for Budget Organizations.

Source: Consultant's analysis.

known financial reporting and treasury management analytical and reporting requirements. This approach is illustrated in Figure 3.

However, three potential problems are identified:

(i) It is not certain that the combined codes will enable all the required analysis for NPSAS and GFS reporting—this requires a detailed study.

(ii) In any event, a bridge table may still be required to enable GFS analysis. Such an approach creates extra work and will always be prone to error or becoming out of date.

(iii) The resulting structure may be relatively complex for staff to use at the point of data entry and will require good IT systems (e.g., pull-down lists based on entity and earlier selections).

It may be preferable to develop a more straightforward COA applied to both budget and accounts, based on the GFS classification in Annex 4 to the Government Finance Statistics Manual 2014 and extended to meet the requirements of IPSAS and specific Uzbekistan requirements. A sub-ledger could provide cash analysis. However, having just adopted a new COA, it is not feasible to make a change at this stage. The requirement is to ensure the newly developed UCOA works and provide the required analysis.

4.1.7 *The Form of National Public Sector Accounting Standards Financial Reports*

NPSAS 3 defines the following financial reports to be produced quarterly unless otherwise stated:

(i) balance sheet (form 1);

(ii) report on results of financial activity (annual);

(iii) budget execution report (form 2);

(iv) debtors and creditors schedule;

(v) budget organization development fund cash flows;

(vi) funds flow statement for medical organizations;

(vii) summary funds flow statement for educational organizations;

(viii) statement of movements on extra-budgetary funds;

(ix) movement of inventories and nonfinancial assets (annual); and

(x) foreign currency movements in budget organizations.

These can be compared to the annual reporting requirements listed in IPSAS 1 as follows:

The reporting formats in NPSAS only partially meet the requirements of IPSAS financial statements (Box). Furthermore, the reports are in the format of internal government reports, and a clearer and more user-friendly format is required for published financial reports to enable transparency.

Box: International Public Sector Accounting Standards Reporting Requirements

(i) Statement of financial position (balance sheet).
(ii) Statement of financial performance (operating statement).
(iii) Statement of changes in net assets/equity.
(iv) Cash flow statement.
(v) Comparison of budget and actual amounts either as a separate additional financial statement or as a budget column in the financial statements.
(vi) Notes comprising a summary of significant accounting policies and other explanations.
(vii) Comparative information with respect to the preceding period.

Source: Consultant's analysis.

Table 10 summarizes the main differences between the proposed reporting formats under NPSAS 3 and the equivalent report under IPSAS where it exists.

As part of the work required on the development of financial reports in accordance with NPSAS during phase 1, the MOF should be assisted in converging mandatory reporting formats under Uzbek regulation with the minimum reporting and disclosure requirements of IPSAS.

Table 10: Comparison of Format Reports

Name of Financial Report/Statement	NPSAS Financial Report	IPSAS Financial Statement
Balance Sheet	**Name: Balance Sheet** Presents the information similarly to IPSAS (current assets/liabilities precede non-current) but lacks explicit references to some accounts on the face of the balance sheet. Does not include all debt liabilities and assets, only those reflected in cash movements. Shows the movement between the beginning and the end of the reporting year.	**Name: Balance Sheet** The IPSAS balance sheet explicitly shows land and intangible assets and prepayments on its face. IPSAS emphasizes the comparison between balances at two year-ends.
Statement of Income and Expenditure	**Name: Report on Results of Financial Activity** Shows the source of funding and expenditure related to those funding sources with few exceptions. Does not analyze expenditure by nature or function. Does not show the minority interest's share of the result on the face of the statement.	**Name: Statement of Financial Performance** Provides a choice between presenting expenditure by function (for consolidated purposes) or nature. Shows the minority interest's share of the result on the face of the statement.
Budget versus Actuals Statement	**Name: Budget Execution Statement** Shows the actual cash and accrued expenditure in the period and the comparison with the final budget. Does not show the original budget.	**Name: Comparison of Budget and Actual Amounts** Can be similar in appearance to its NPSAS equivalent, except it also shows the original budget as well as the final budget.
Debtors and Creditors	**Name: Information on Debtors and Creditors** Analyzes key accounts receivable/ payable at the end of each quarter.	No such statement exists, but the same information as in the NPSAS report could be shown as a disclosure note under IPSAS.
Equity Statement	Does not exist under NPSAS.	**Name: Statement of Changes in Net Assets or Equity**
Cash Flow Statement	Does not exist under NPSAS.	**Name: Cash Flow Statement**
Source and Application of Funds	**Name: Budget Organization Development Fund Cash Flows** **Name: Funds Flow Statement for Medical Organizations** **Name: Summary Funds Flow Statement for Medical Organizations** **Name: Statement of Movements on Extra Budgetary Funds** All the above are simple statements showing opening and closing cash balances, receipts to and payments from funds controlled by the reporting budget organizations. Below each of these simple funds flow statements, total expenses are analyzed by detailed nature of expense, both in cash and accrual terms.	Such reports do not exist under IPSAS, but the NPSAS statements are similar in concept to mini cash flow statements (operating flows only) and analyze expenditure in some detail by nature.
Inventories and Fixed Assets	**Name: Movements of Non-financial Assets** Shows gross asset values at the beginning of the year, acquisitions, disposals, amounts (of inventories) expensed, and balances at year-end.	No such statement exists, but the same information report could be shown as a disclosure note under IPSAS. IPSAS disclosures for fixed assets would show movements on the cumulative depreciation account in addition to what is shown under NPSAS.
Foreign Currency Funds Flow	As for the Source and Application of Funds Reports above but denominated in foreign currency.	As for the comment above with respect to the Source and Application of Funds Reports.

IPSAS = International Public Sector Accounting Standards, NPSAS = National Public Sector Accounting Standards.

Source: Consultant's analysis.

CONSOLIDATED FINANCIAL REPORTING FOR THE PUBLIC SECTOR

5

5.1 The Reason for Consolidation

The ultimate objective of the IPSAS financial reporting framework is to consolidate the entities' financial reports within its scope to produce a whole-of-government view of financial status and performance. To achieve such an overall view of government accounting, public sector entities reporting under IPSAS often have to be consolidated with public corporations reporting under IFRS. Thus, consolidation of financial statements prepared under compatible but different frameworks is a common feature of the public sector financial reporting landscape.

In the current context, with the non-budget sector standard-setting and financial reporting framework already well established, it may not be feasible in the short term to require a relatively large number of non-profit-seeking SOEs to come over to an IPSAS-based framework in the earliest stages of its development. The right to define which entities adopt NPSAS remains a jurisdictional one.

5.2 Scope of the Consolidation

The IPSAS financial reporting framework is developed for public sector entities that do not seek to make a profit, and it is recognized by the Board that sets the standards (IPSASB) that public sector entities of a commercial nature with profit-seeking objectives are likely to either report in accordance with IFRS or other nationally developed financial reporting standards for profit-seeking entities.[11]

The government's current plan is that NPSAS should be adopted by entities within the consolidated budget, which includes subnational authorities under the central government's control. This is a sensible and feasible starting point for phase 1 of the proposed road map. However, the consolidated budget is a more limited scope for adopting IPSAS than required under either IPSAS or GFS.

GFS is mentioned in this connection because IPSAS explicitly attempts to achieve consistency with GFS so that IPSAS and GFS reports are as similar as possible. It is also worth noting that IPSAS 22 explicitly allows additional financial reports under IPSAS per the GFS scope. According to IPSAS, such reports are in addition to, not instead, the IPSAS scope as defined above.

[11] Paragraph 1.8 of the Conceptual Framework for General Purpose Financial Reporting by Public Sector Entities identifies a wide range of public sector entities for which IPSASs are designed. IPSASB. 2014. *Conceptual Framework for General Purpose Financial Reporting by Public Sector Entities.*

To prepare financial statements for the whole of the government,

(i) IPSAS consolidation is determined by control—all entities controlled, either directly or indirectly, by the government are within the scope of IPSAS-compliant government financial reports; and

(ii) GFS consolidation is determined by sectors, and the main consolidated financial reports are, on the whole, of the GGS.

A major practical difference between these two approaches is that, unlike IPSAS, GFS does not set itself the objective of consolidating the financial statements of SOEs with commercial objectives (or "public corporations" as they are known in GFS) within the accounts of the government. IPSAS refers to these entities as "commercial public sector entities."

It is noticeable from Figure 4 that what needs to be added to the current scope of NPSAS, if it aspires to be consistent with IPSAS, are the non-profit-seeking SOEs.

Figure 4: Different Parameters of Government Consolidated Financial Report for International Public Sector Accounting Standards and Government Financial Statistics

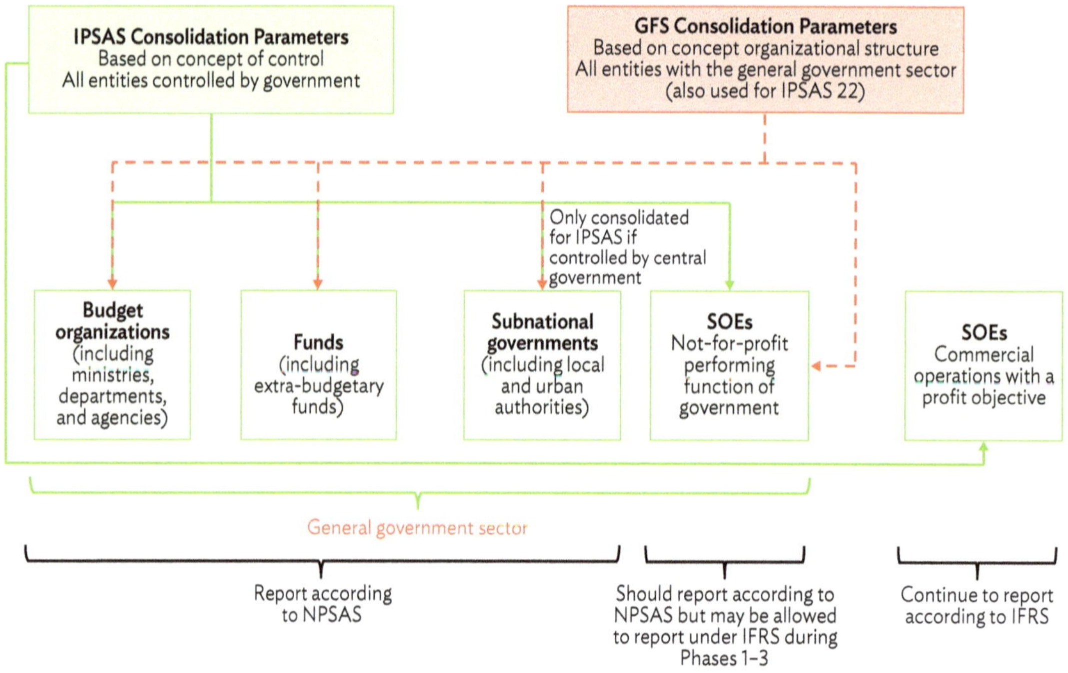

GFS = government financial statistics, IFRS = international financial reporting standards, IPSAS = International Public Sector Accounting Standards, NPSAS = National Public Sector Accounting Standards, SOE = state-owned enterprise.

Source: Consultant's analysis.

The road map recommends consolidated reporting should be extended as follows::

(i) Phase 1: consolidated budget;

(ii) Phase 2: general government sector (GFS and IPSAS 22); and

(iii) Phase 3: all controlled entities (IPSAS 35).

This phasing is illustrated in Figure 5.

Figure 5: Alternative Consolidation Parameters

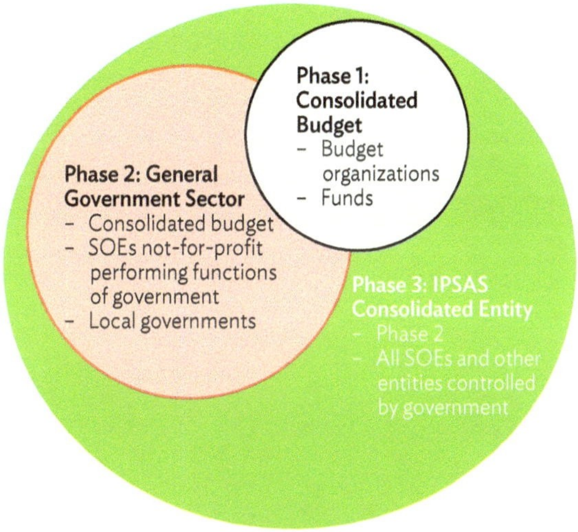

IPSAS = International Public Sector Accounting Standards, SOE = state-owned enterprise.

Notes:

- The above analysis assumes there are no nonresident SOEs controlled by the government as these are not part of the government sector for government financial statistics reporting but are included for IPSAS reporting.
- It is also assumed that subnational levels of government meet the definition of being controlled by the central government; if not, they are excluded from the consolidation for the purposes of IPSAS but included for government financial statistics in the general government sector.

Source: Consultant's analysis.

5.2.1 Phase 1: Defining the Potential Consolidation Boundary

The phase 1 consolidation will be of entities within the consolidated budget. Later phases of convergence with IPSAS could embrace firstly the GGS (consistent with GFS and IPSAS 22 parameters) and eventually all controlled entities for full IPSAS-compliant consolidation.

At present, all SOEs in Uzbekistan come under the same legal instrument, which defines them as commercial enterprises and requires them to prepare financial statements in accordance with NAS based on IFRS. These financial statements are submitted to the State Tax Service and Committee for Statistics every quarter.

It is estimated that there are approximately 1,700 SOEs and 150 limited liability companies with government equity shares of more than 50%.

The financial reporting regime the SOEs come under is well established since the first such national standard governing the SOEs' production of financial statements has existed since 1998. The Law of Accounting, which prescribes this financial reporting framework, was first introduced in 1996.

The formats of the SOEs' financial statements currently used for SOE financial reporting differ in several key respects from those proposed for NPSAS financial reporting and even from IPSAS reports. Nevertheless, a method will eventually have to be found to map the financial results and positions of all public sector entities within the scope of IPSAS to a set of consolidated reports.

It is not unusual for the IPSAS financial reporting framework to have to deal with the fact that some larger public entities already report under IFRS, so to achieve whole-of-public sector accounting, IPSAS entities in the government sector must be consolidated with public corporations reporting under IFRS. In the case of Uzbekistan, this problem is particularly acute: a relatively large number of SOEs, even not-for-profit entities, who would usually be expected to adopt IPSAS, have long since prepared financial statements under NAS.

Therefore, the government needs to decide whether to maintain these split financial reporting frameworks or force non-budget public sector entities to converge on IPSAS.

5.2.2 Phase 2: Aggregating the Financial Reports of Entities

Regardless of the eventual scope of IPSAS, the process of consolidating reporting entities is simple in principle, but, in an extensive network of interrelated entities, can become relatively complicated in practice unless it is automated. Where entities are within the scope of a single IT system with a common COA, such as those within the consolidated budget, aggregating the financial reports of all entities involved is potentially straightforward if accounting policies are applied consistently by the entities to be consolidated.

The consolidation process is more complicated for entities such as SOEs that are outside the scope of the same accounting system. Usually, this is achieved by entering information from the audited financial reports of each entity into a spreadsheet or specialized consolidation software. For this process to go smoothly, the entities' financial reports to be consolidated must be in a standard format. This could be a problem if the production of the financial reports compatible with NAS reports is seriously delayed or does not correspond in format and content with those prepared under NPSAS. The latter situation may arise and be exacerbated by any differences in accounting policies adopted for material elements of the financial statements by SOEs and entities within the scope of the consolidated budget.

5.2.3 Phase 3: Eliminating Flows and Balances between Entities

A fundamental component of consolidating is eliminating flows between entities to avoid double counting. For example, if Ministry X pays taxes to the Treasury, then these should be canceled out in the consolidation.

This presents several issues such as the following:

(i) All flows and balances between entities in the consolidation must be identified, and a process established for their elimination in the consolidated financial reports.

(ii) Inevitably, there will be a difference between what one entity thinks it owns and what another entity thinks it is owed—procedures must exist to resolve such problems.

(iii) The fact that some flows and balances are in cash and the corresponding flows in other entities are on an accrual basis.

(iv) The setting of materiality limits so that flows and balances below a specified level are ignored.

Eliminating inter-entity flows and balances is conceptually simple but practically difficult, especially when there are different accounting bases and sub-consolidations. It is best dealt with through an automated system that flags inter-entity flows, but this becomes more difficult to achieve when several different IT systems are in use.

The problem becomes especially complex when there are sub-consolidations, for example, a budget organization consolidates a group of entities under its control, which are then all consolidated into the government-consolidated financial reports, as illustrated in Figure 6.

Figure 7 illustrates the problem with just six entities. The complexity grows exponentially with multiple entities. Elimination is only feasible using IT systems. But the first requirement is to establish systems to identify such inter-entity flows and balances, and how to deal with the inevitable issue when the balances, as recorded by different entities, do not match.

Figure 6: Illustration of the Complexity of Elimination of All Flows and Balances between Entities

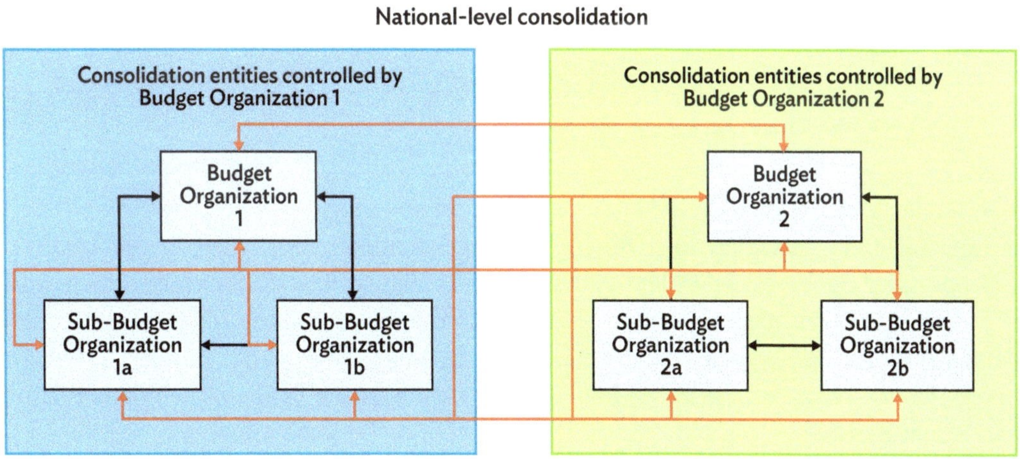

Note: Red lines indicate possible flows and balances between all entities that must be eliminated on consolidation.
Source: Consultant's analysis.

Possible approaches are as follows:

(i) For Phase 1, the problem will be small and can be dealt with manually using spreadsheets or a simple database.

(ii) For Phase 2, assuming a much more extensive range of entities is to be consolidated, "consolidation forms" to be completed by each entity within the scope of the consolidation can be used to identify inter-entity flows and balances. At this stage, specialist consolidation software will be required.

(iii) Beyond Phase 3, the issue should be addressed as part of the broader issue of implementing IFMIS.

In practice, ignoring minor flows and balances as immaterial will be necessary. The whole of this process requires planning, design, and training.

5.2.4 *Information Technology Systems*

As indicated earlier, the success of the consolidation depends on IT systems. However, the IT systems will only function correctly if designed according to appropriate specifications. These must address the following issues:

(i) Inter-entity balances must be identified in the computer system, using either designated codes or some other system of "flagging" such items.

(ii) There must be rules for the process to be followed when cross flows or balances do not match different entities' accounts.

(iii) Rules are required to deal with the mix of cash and accrual flows and balances.

It is essential that such specifications are appropriately documented and that the system is tested with the full volume of entities before "live" implementation.

5.3 Integrating National Public Sector Accounting Standards and National Accounting Standards (International Financial Reporting Standards) Reporting

As noted earlier, all SOEs in Uzbekistan currently report according to NAS based on IFRS. This will become an issue during consolidation if the formats or content of the SOEs' and budget sector entities' financial reports are significantly different. Although IPSAS are based on IFRS and consistent in principle, the NPSAS have involved adapting IPSAS. Therefore, to minimize potential obstacles to consolidating the financial results of public sector entities, it will be necessary to review NAS developing NPSAS in the same subject area to ensure consistency between the standards and increase the chances of mapping the reports successfully.

It is strongly recommended that at an early stage of drafting any new NPSAS, MOF accounting methodology specialists consider the accounting policies permitted by NAS in the same subject area. As stated earlier but worth repeating here, by making the accounting policies within the respective sets of accounting standards consistent, the chances of successfully consolidating the financial reports of SOEs and budget sector entities prepared under different financial reporting frameworks are increased.

PROJECT MANAGEMENT AND RISKS

6

6.1 Project Management

The adoption of IPSAS standards and implementation of NPSAS is a major project that extends well beyond the MOF and Treasury and requires a dedicated management team—a PMU—with sufficient authority and resources to drive the implementation of the required reforms. The focus of the PMU is project management and coordination, distinct from an M&E role that focuses on the quality of the financial statements produced under the new accounting framework.

A formal project management structure involving a high-level Steering Committee, the PMU, and M&E Unit should be instituted. The PMU would coordinate training activities through a dedicated training team located at the MOF Training Centre. Awareness and communication would be a joint responsibility of the Steering Committee and the PMU, and the M&E function would also report to these bodies. A proposed structure is shown in Figure 7.

Figure 7: Project Management Structure

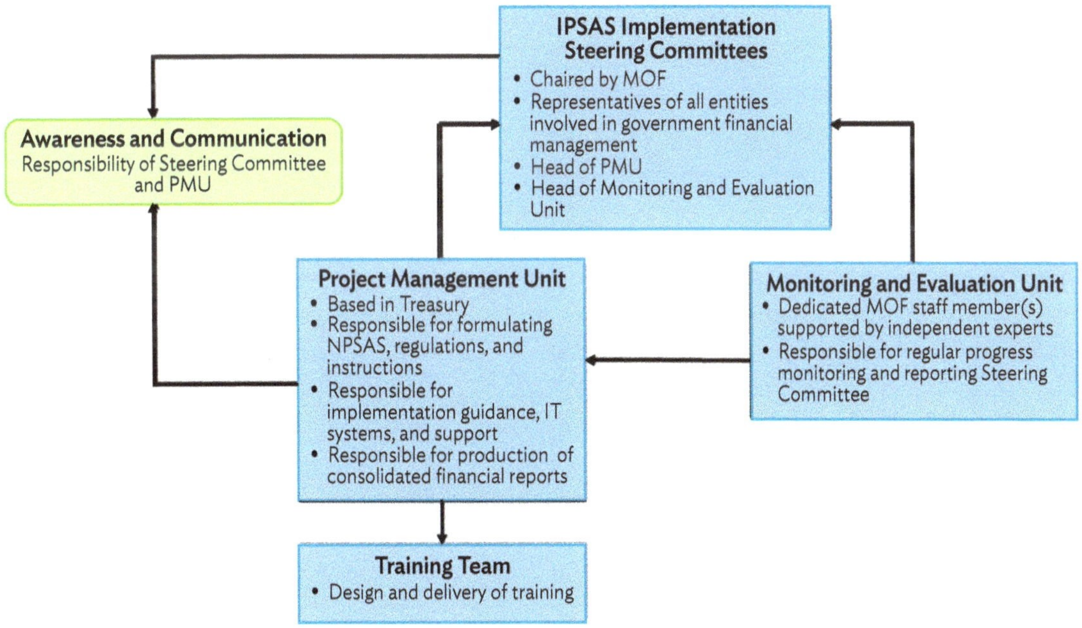

IPSAS = International Public Sector Accounting Standards, IT = information technology, MOF = Ministry of Finance, NPSAS = National Public Sector Accounting Standards, PMU = Project Management Unit.

Source: Consultant's analysis.

This management structure is urgently required and should ideally be fully implemented and embedded during phase 1. It should be noted that the M&E Unit shown in Figure 8 should be supported by an external independent consultant or agency facilitating periodic progress checks.

Another body not shown in the diagram but having an important role to play in the development of NPSAS but not entirely within the MOF structure is the proposed technical committee reporting to the MOF (project Steering Committee and PMU) and comprising technically qualified people drawn from several relevant domains who review each new draft NPSAS and comment on it.

6.2 Risks and Mitigation Actions

There are seven significant areas of risk associated with this reform program.

6.2.1 Risk 1: Changes to the Proposed Road Map Schedule

Changes to the timing or scope of the implementation of IPSAS set out in this road map may be occasioned by any of the following:

(i) longer implementation periods for the individual standards and road map phases overall;

(ii) changes to the consolidation boundary; or

(iii) a change in the government's PFM policies concerning the full implementation of IPSAS.

In addition to the mitigation measures suggested in the following paragraphs, the risk of slippage and failure to deliver the expected scope can be controlled to some extent by tight project management on the part of the PMU as well as regular communication between the beneficiary and expert advisers so that prompt and targeted actions minimize the potential adverse impacts from any internal or environmental issues.

6.2.2 Risk 2: Resistance to Change

Any reform inevitably meets resistance, either because of a general suspicion or even apathy toward change or the perceived impact on individuals. To address such issues, it will be necessary for the IPSAS implementation project to move beyond the MOF to involve all stakeholders across government, politicians, and eventually civil society organizations.

High-level political support will be required to emphasize the importance of the reforms, together with appropriate regulatory changes. Various communication tools should be used to communicate with all the stakeholders. This should be the day-to-day responsibility of the PMU, overseen by the project Steering Committee, and will require staff with an aptitude for communication and general knowledge of financial accounting and reporting.

6.2.3 Risk 3: Staff Unable to Perform Tasks

The reforms will require staff at all levels to perform new and often more demanding tasks. In particular, the accrual basis IPSAS framework, with its extensive disclosure requirements, will challenge accountants' knowledge across the government. It will require a different way of thinking and deploying deeper skills in accounting and financial reporting. Part of the solution is to provide adequate well-designed training and continue supporting them through the implementation process. Still, it is also evident that technical knowledge and analytical ability will need to be brought into the finance functions by recruiting new, qualified specialists over the extended duration of the implementation.

Developing the capacity for delivering IPSAS financial statements requires several phases (implementing the standards themselves), from the initial comprehensive training needs analysis and developing a credible training plan in the short term to creating a professional cadre of accountants in the long term.

The training needs analysis can be done with specialist advisers' help. The design and implementation of the training plan will be the primary responsibility of the training center under the control of the MOF. The implementation will also require sufficiently numerous and qualified dedicated trainers, competent professionals in M&E roles to periodically point out quality gaps, and a more rounded contingent of practitioner accountants preparing correct and compliant financial statements. It will require more than training existing staff, over time new talent needs to be recruited into key positions, both within the MOF and the larger reporting entities.

6.2.4 Risk 4: Systems and Procedures Do Not Function as Intended

The planned reforms require extensive procedural changes, new or upgraded IT systems, and new roles for staff. Inevitably, some of these will function differently than intended. The changes are far-reaching and complex, and problems must be anticipated.

All systems, especially IT systems, must be thoroughly tested with the volume of entities and transactions envisaged. Testing should be a structured process with test results evaluated and signed off by management when completed satisfactorily.

During initial implementation, all processes and results should be monitored, and any issues identified at an early stage so that corrective action can be taken (see section 6.2.1).

6.2.5 Risk 5: Inadequate Management of Change

The consultant's analysis of risks emphasizes the need for a dedicated high-quality management team with authority to make decisions affecting all government areas. A PMU is urgently required with adequate staffing for the tasks to be performed and sufficient authority to act.

A systematic approach to reconfiguring, upgrading, and testing IT systems in line with changed accounting and financial reporting requirements necessitated by the new NPSAS should also be adopted. Each task should have a due date and quality criteria in line with project management best practice.

6.2.6 Risk 6: International Public Sector Accounting Standards Coverage May Be Restricted

If the government does not permit SOEs to report under NPSAS (switching from NAS based on IFRS), the scope of the IPSAS implementation may ultimately be restricted to the entities within the consolidated budget until or unless the policy changes.

The most effective mitigation, in this case, would be to ensure that financial reports for the whole public sector are consolidated under a separate process managed by the MOF.

6.2.7 Risk 7: Better Financial Information Does Not Lead to Improved Decision-Making

The government requires a significant effort of time and financial resources to move toward accruals accounting based on IPSAS. New information will be produced, but experience from similar developments in other countries suggests that sometimes this is seen as a technical accounting issue rather than one that is primarily aimed at improving decision-making or holding public bodies to account for their performance.

To mitigate against this risk, it is essential that decision-makers at a high level of government, in particular the Cabinet of Ministers and the legislature, are actively involved in the ongoing evolution of NPSAS/IPSAS and given detailed guidance on an ongoing basis regarding how best to use the enhanced information they will have in the future to make better-informed decisions.

6.3 Monitoring and Evaluation

A dedicated M&E Unit consisting of one or more in-house full-time equivalents (FTEs) (depending on need) supported by independent external consultants should conduct monitoring of the quality of financial reporting under NPSAS as it evolves and reports its findings to the PMU and Steering Committee.

6.4 Internal and External Audit

The 2018 Public Expenditure and Financial Accountability (PEFA) gave a score of D+ to the internal audit. This reflects the fact that modern internal audit approaches still need to be implemented. However, the MOF is tasked with developing an internal audit function for the state budget sector.

The conclusion reached by the 2018 PEFA was that the focus of internal auditors within the ministries in which it was established was on compliance with budget regulations, including the appropriateness of budget spending and the accuracy of the reporting of budget execution. Internal audits do not yet work in the MOF. Instead, a Control and Revision Unit (CRU) continues to operate and "employs elements of [the] internal audit function in the way they describe their job."[12]

[12] 2018 PEFA Performance Assessment Report, paragraph 417. This unit is now called Department of State Financial Control.

The CRU based in the central administration of the MOF sees its role as policing compliance with the law and budget code, both of which are referred to in the preamble of each NPSAS. Given this legal compliance connection, the CRU would be ready to verify the correct application of the NPSAS. However, it should be emphasized that the CRU has a predominantly compliance focus and that developing the MOF's dedicated reviewing staff and the ability to fully consider the technical and qualitative aspects of international financial reporting will take more time than is probably appreciated.

A modern internal audit function and the in-house Department of State Financial Control (i.e., CRU) within the MOF could be important in ensuring the implementation of the IPSAS reforms. It should work closely with the M&E function to ensure that progress reports reflect the actual situation and to identify areas where further action and support are required.

It will be important that the Chamber of Accounts, as the external auditor of public entities, provides an audit opinion of the new financial reports in the format prescribed by the International Organization of Supreme Audit Institutions. This will require significant upgrading of the capacity of the Chamber of Accounts. Experience from many other countries (e.g., the United Kingdom and France) is that the involvement of the Supreme Audit Institution in the development of accruals accounting is a critical factor for ensuring a successful transition to full accruals accounting.

6.5 Costs of Integrated Financial Management Information System Implementation

Implementation costs vary with the scope and scale size of the implementation. However, it is possible to get an approximate idea of the costs to be expected for implementing a system with a given scope, from existing data on completed projects, by plotting the contracted cost of actual systems implementation against the number of end users (used as a proxy for scale size of the system) that are connected to the system.

The World Bank has done this for 10 World Bank-financed IFMIS projects that involve the implementation of a commercial off-the-shelf package.[13] The results indicate that, as a broad parameter, it is safe to assume that commercial off-the-shelf implementation costs would be about $15,000 per user. If the number of users is approximately 2,000, then implementation of the new IFMIS would cost around $30 million.

[13] World Bank. 2014. *A Handbook on Financial Management Information Systems for Government*. Washington, DC.

6.6 Costs of the Implementation of National Public Sector Accounting Standards (Phases 1–3 Inclusive)

The main areas of costs for the development and dissemination of NPSASs closely aligned with IPSAS are set out below and summarized in Table 11.

6.6.1 Technical Support to Develop and Implement National Public Sector Accounting Standards

The MOF's budget organizations' methodology department has completed a significant task with the formal adoption of 12 NPSAS. However, moving to the full implementation of IPSAS requires the support of a dedicated project team, starting with a PMU, consisting of local resources and being able to call on the assistance of national and international IPSAS experts. Although there is considerable expertise within Uzbekistan, the range of reforms will require external advisory support, and the expected costs of these resources is shown in Table 11.

6.6.2 Information Technology Systems Upgrades to Integrated Financial Management Information System

To achieve NPSAS implementation, the existing IT systems will need to be upgraded. Beyond the first phase of the implementation scheduled for 2020–2021 inclusive, if the complex consolidation of a broader scope of entities than the consolidated budget is to be automated, an integrated IFMIS will be required. This will require the specification, acquisition, and implementation of new IT systems, which in turn will require substantial cash investment in hardware; software development; and program licenses, software maintenance, and user training.

In the estimates shown in Table 11, the overall cost of developing a large new system needs to be factored in. Instead, provision is made for the cost of upgrades to existing software systems as well as the development of functional and technical specifications of the proposed new IFMIS.

A further $460,000 is allocated to the implementation support of the new system once it has gone live until the end of the road map (2030).

6.6.3 Training Costs

Training will be a substantial cost element during all three phases of IPSAS implementation for which estimates are provided. It will include technical training for MOF staff, user training for all accounting staff and external auditors, and instruction on developing and enabling new reporting formats and accounting processes in the IT systems. It should also guide decision-makers on best using the new information produced.

Table 11: Estimated Costs of the Implementation of National Public Sector Accounting Standards (Phases 1–3 Inclusive)

Cost Element	Units	Per Unit	No. of Units	Total Cost
Operational support				
Project Management Unit (2 full-time staff)	Month	$2,000	144	$288,000.00
Monitoring and Evaluation	Month	$2,000	43	$86,000.00
Travel, equipment, and subsistence	Estimate	$20,000	1	$20,000.00
Technical support				
International advisory services	Month	$20,000	12	$240,000.00
National advisory services	Month	$2,000	72	$144,000.00
Travel, equipment, and subsistence	Estimate	$100,000	1	$100,000.00
Subtotal				$878,000.00
IT systems upgrades				
New IFMIS specification				
International (1 person)	Months	$20,000	3	$60,000.00
National (1 person)	Months	$2,000	6	$12,000.00
Upgrade software, including necessary tweaks	Months	$10,000	6	$60,000.00
Hardware improvement (server)	Estimate	$200,000	1	$200,000.00
New IFMIS implementation support				
International (1 person)	Months	$20,000	12	$240,000.00
National (1 person)	Months	$2,000	60	$120,000.00
Travel and subsistence	Estimate	$100,000	1	$100,000.00
Subtotal				$792,000.00
Training costs				
Trainers				
International (2 persons)	Months	$20,000	24	$480,000.00
National (6 trainers)	Months	$2,000	144	$288,000.00
Travel, equipment, and subsistence	Estimate	$200,000	1	$200,000.00
Training center and mobile training unit	Estimate	$100,000	1	$100,000.00
Subtotal				$1,068,000.00
Other costs				
Public relations and stakeholder awareness	Estimate	$50,000	1	$50,000.00
Contribution to other dissemination costs	Estimate	$56,000	1	$56,000.00
Subtotal				$106,000.00
GRAND TOTAL				**$2,844,000.00**

IFMIS = integrated financial management information system, IT = information technology.

Source: Consultant's analysis.

6.6.4 Government Costs

The government will also incur costs in connection with this project, such as those to fund physical or virtual training facilities, to print and distribute learning materials or make them available online, make changes to the IT configuration of existing systems, and to pay staff per diems and the travel costs of trainers. Internal costs, such as the salaries of those specialists who join dedicated project teams of in-house resources working alongside external advisers, are also relevant to the complete costing of this project. However, these costs are not factored into the overall estimates in Table 11.

Although estimates of implementation costs to be borne by the state budget are not included in the costings shown in Table 11, it should be emphasized that to adopt NPSAS and then IPSAS correctly, each major reporting entity such as a ministry, large agency, or municipal administration will almost certainly need to create an internal task force, PMU, or similar special unit to oversee the implementation. If the right people are selected for this role, they will be able to manage it within their normal work schedules, and it will, therefore, not be necessary to recruit new employees to backfill the positions left by the PMU members. A senior accountant could be designated part-time PMU head and form a project team from existing accounting staff to manage to introduce each new NPSAS. With the expected learning effect, the burden on the NPSAS implementation oversight team would reduce over time. If large reporting entities felt that their existing staff needed help to cope unaided with the demands of NPSAS, a cautious estimate of additional resources required could be one new FTE, for which they would have to make allowance in their expenditure budgets.

From 2020 onward, the MOF will be heavily relied upon to review financial statements in greater detail than hitherto and to provide more remote technical (help-desk type) assistance to reporting entities. To increase internal capacity to cope with the extra burden (or reduce the risk of failure due to lack of capacity), the MOF should make provision in its staffing budgets for resources at least matching the two FTEs for centralized PMU and one part-time oversight M&E operative proposed as the contribution from the externally funded project illustrated in Table 11. This would give the MOF additional resources to recruit and train its own team of specialists working alongside the project and maximize knowledge transfer into the MOF.

6.6.5 Other Costs

Provision for the cost of raising stakeholder awareness of the proposed reforms contained in the road map is recommended, as is a contribution to other dissemination costs that the MOF will necessarily incur throughout the implementation period. This funding is intended to raise the MOF's digital capability to disseminate training materials to users across the country and pay for translating preexisting learning materials that could be used during the development of NPSAS.

www.ingramcontent.com/pod-product-compliance
Lightning Source LLC
Chambersburg PA
CBHW041759220926
51847CB00014B/256
* 9 7 8 9 2 9 2 7 0 2 8 6 1 *